Fermented Vegetables

The Ultimate Guide to Fermentation and Pickling Techniques and Recipes for Beginners and Beyond

Tables of Contents

Introduction

There's nothing quite like the sour crunch of a perfectly fermented pickle. Whether it is tangy dill spears on a sandwich, crispy kimchi on a taco, or a fizzy swig of kvass, fermented foods add a kick of flavor. But if the world of pickling and fermentation seems daunting, don't worry. This book makes it easy and fun.

Fermented Vegetables is an inviting guide to unlocking the flavorful art of fermenting vegetables at home. Even if you've never pickled more than a few cucumbers from the garden, this book will turn you into a fermentation aficionado in no time.

The book begins by demystifying the simple science behind vegetable fermentation. Using natural bacteria like Lactobacillus, the fermentation process transforms and preserves vegetables, extending the shelf life exponentially. As the good bacteria break down starches and sugars, they impart their signature tangy sourness and delightful crunch. Fermented foods become packed with beneficial probiotics, but beyond preservation, fermentation unlocks new depths of flavors and nutrition. From sour dills to fiery kimchi, many iconic foods rely on fermentation.

In this book, you'll learn hands-on techniques for fermenting classic pickled vegetables in your kitchen. Step-by-step instructions and visual guides make the process unintimidating for first-timers. You'll gain confidence mastering easy fermented staples like sauerkraut, dilly carrots, and pickled jalapeños, and before you know it, you'll be equipped to ferment and pickle a variety of vegetables.

The book goes beyond basic fermentation to offer shortcuts for quickly pickling vegetables without a drawn-out process. Quick pickles and refrigerator methods let you infuse vibrant flavors into veggies within hours. Consider it an instant upgrade to salads, sandwiches, snacking, and more. You'll find recipes and techniques for fermenting unique vegetables like cauliflowers, radishes, beets, and carrots into tasty, fermented concoctions.

As your skills advance, you'll learn techniques for handling larger batches, fermenting in crocks, managing ideal temperatures, and preventing common troubleshooting issues. Equipped with in-depth knowledge and pointers, you'll consistently produce properly fermented vegetables bursting with flavor.

More than a mere how-to guide, this book inspires you to get creative with homemade flavors. You'll discover ideas for incorporating bright pickled vegetables into everyday meals, drinks, sauces, and more. With the power of fermentation, the possibilities for homemade flavors are endless.

Whether you're a newcomer looking to develop a tasty new skill or a seasoned fermenter seeking to expand your repertoire, this book makes pickling and fermenting fun, unintimidating, and delicious. Follow the step-by-step instructions as you gain confidence, abilities, and a taste for tangy fermented creations. Soon, your kitchen will be fully equipped to transform vegetables into funky ferments that dazzle family and friends.

Chapter 1: Introduction to Fermented Vegetables

This chapter introduces you to fermentation, an age-old technique that transforms vegetables into tangy, crunchy foods. You'll learn the science behind how fermentation works through beneficial bacteria. These microbes act on sugars and starches in veggies to naturally preserve them. It extends shelf life dramatically while boosting nutrients.

1.   Many iconic foods depend on fermentation. Source: https://unsplash.com/photos/three-jars-filled-with-different-types-of-food-JzY97tKL_oM?utm_content=creditShareLink&utm_medium=refer ral&utm_source=unsplash

Fermentation unlocks incredible new flavors and textures, providing vegetables that signature tangy sourness and delightful crunch. From kimchi to pickles, many iconic foods depend on fermentation. This chapter outlines the health perks of eating fermented vegetables, from gut health to better digestion.

Overview of Fermentation and Pickling

Fermentation uses beneficial microorganisms like yeasts and bacteria to transform and preserve food. During fermentation, these microbes feed on sugars and starches in the food, producing acids, gases, and alcohol as byproducts. The buildup of these compounds inhibits spoilage while imparting new flavors and textures.

Fermentation extends the shelf life of foods and enhances their nutritional value. It can generate B vitamins, omega-3 fatty acids, and antioxidants. Additionally, fermented foods contain probiotics, beneficial bacteria that support gut health and immunity when consumed.

The Science of Fermentation

Fermentation often relies on the microorganisms already present in the food or introduced from the environment. For instance, grapes harbor yeasts on their skins that get the wine fermentation process going. However, in many cases, starter cultures are intentionally added to kickstart and control fermentation. This is done with yogurt, which uses specific strains of bacteria. The microbes and length of fermentation impact the end product's flavor profile and texture.

Here's an overview of the fermentation science:

- It starts when vegetables (or other foods) are submerged in a brine solution. The brine has little oxygen but lots of salt.

- Salt stops dangerous microbes from growing while letting good bacteria thrive. These microbes are naturally on the food or added as a starter culture.

- The bacteria munch on sugars in the veggies, changing them into lactic acid, carbon dioxide, and other compounds. This lowers the pH and gives ferments that sour taste.

- The acidic environment prevents spoilage by blocking harmful microbes. The carbon dioxide usually makes the vegetables fizzy.

- Over time, enzymes break down plant cells, softening the texture. Complex flavors build up as byproducts like alcohols, esters, and peptides accumulate.

- Once the acidity and flavor are right, fermented vegetables can be chilled to slow fermentation. The cold and the brine will preserve them for months.

While it seems simple, cabbage turning into sauerkraut involves a complex microbial dance. Certain bacteria are vital in fermenting vegetables. Known as lactic acid bacteria (LAB), common players are:

1. Lactobacillus

The most important LAB genus includes L. plantarum and L. mesenteroides. Lactobacillus are rod-shaped and can handle high acid. They efficiently change sugars into lactic acid, even in very acidic conditions below pH 4. This acidification gives many ferments their tang and blocks pathogens. Some types, like L. plantarum, are heterofermentative, meaning they produce lactic acid plus alcohol and carbon dioxide.

2. Leuconostoc

It generates carbon dioxide, which makes vegetables fizzy and produces lactic and acetic acid. Leuconostoc is more common early on. They are heterofermenters, turning sugars into lactate plus acetate, ethanol, carbon dioxide, and other substances. The carbon dioxide makes some ferments bubbly.

3. Pediococcus

Pediococcus are home fermenters, mostly making lactic acid. They can handle very acidic conditions down to pH 3.2. Pediococcus keeps acidifying and developing flavor even when it's too acidic for other bacteria.

Beyond making acids, LAB also brings key enzymes that break down tough plant fibers. Fermentation enriches and transforms nutrients in vegetables through bioconversion. LAB generates B vitamins, antioxidants, and other essential compounds as they change food molecularly.

These LAB work together to lower pH, create new flavors, and beat pathogens. Within a week and in the right conditions, LAB can acidify vegetables to a pH below 4.6, which is safe for lengthy storage. The time needed depends on temperature, salt level, and vegetable type. For instance, cabbage for sauerkraut acidifies faster than cucumbers for pickles.

Other bacteria like Enterococcus, Lactococcus, and Weissella sometimes help out. Wild yeasts can also play supporting roles. Natural bacteria on various vegetables also differ.

What Is Pickling?

Pickling refers to preserving foods in a brine solution, usually water, salt, vinegar, and an acid like lemon juice. The high acidity and salinity of pickling brine inhibit microbial growth while infusing foods with tangy flavors. Pickling also encompasses food preservation in oil or alcohol rather than brine.

A variety of fruits, vegetables, proteins, and condiments are commonly pickled, including cucumbers, cabbages (sauerkraut), eggs, meats, relishes, and olives. Pickling may or may not involve fermentation. Quick pickles, like pickled cucumbers and onions, rely on the brine's acidity for preservation and don't undergo fermentation. On the other hand, fermented pickles rely on lactic acid produced by bacteria to preserve the food.

One major benefit of pickling is that it retains, and in some cases improves, the nutritional content of food. Pickling enables preserving seasonal produce like summer's bounty of cucumbers to enjoy year-round. By infusing foods with lively flavors, pickling makes meals more appetizing and varied.

Basic Principles of Fermentation and Pickling

Several key factors enable fermentation and pickling to transform and successfully preserve food over extended periods. Here is an overview of the basic principles of fermentation and pickling:

1. Controlling Microorganisms

- Discouraging spoilage while encouraging beneficial organisms is key.

- Washing produce removes surface microbes.

- Salt inhibits unwanted microbial growth.

- Adding starter cultures crowds out undesirable microbes.

- Acidic environments inhibit pathogens. Anaerobic fermentation prevents mold.

2. Acidity

- Lowering pH creates an inhospitable environment for spoilage organisms.

- Lactic acid produced by fermentation increases acidity.

- Adding vinegar or lemon juice lowers the pH of pickling brine.

3. Salting

- Salt draws out cellular moisture, inhibiting microbial growth.

- It toughens vegetable cell walls, keeping texture crunchy.

- Salt suppresses undesirable microbes, giving desired organisms an advantage.

4. Sugars and Starches

- Carbohydrates fuel fermentation.

- Vegetables, grains, and fruit contain sugars and starch that microorganisms convert into acids, gases, and alcohol.
- Salt enhances this breakdown.

5. Anaerobic Conditions

- Excluding oxygen prevents mold growth and allows anaerobic bacteria and yeast to thrive in fermentation.
- Keeping vegetables submerged beneath brine activates this in pickling.
- Airlock lids maintain anaerobic conditions during fermentation.

6. Time and Temperature

- Fermentation and pickling progress faster in warmer temperatures.
- Cooler temperatures slow the process.
- The length of fermentation or pickling time affects flavor and preservation.

7. Moisture Content

- Vegetables must have enough moisture for fermentation.
- Salt draws out moisture from cell walls.
- Adding whey or pickling brine provides moisture.
- Drying, as in dry-cured sausages, inhibits spoilage microbes.

While salt, acid, sugars, microbes, and moisture content play varying roles, controlling these factors enables the successful transformation of fresh ingredients into safely preserved, flavorful products.

Common Fermented and Pickled Foods

Many foods you eat regularly are produced via fermentation or pickling. Here is an overview of some of the most popular categories:

Sauerkraut and Kimchi

These are cabbage-based side dishes enlivened by fermentation. For sauerkraut, shredded cabbage is salted to draw out moisture and then fermented by lactic acid bacteria, giving it a tangy sour flavor. Kimchi showcases fermented cabbage with added seasonings like garlic, ginger, and chili pepper for a spicy kick. Both provide probiotics.

Yogurt

Milk fermented by bacterial cultures becomes yogurt, valued for its thick, creamy texture, tanginess, and probiotic content. Yogurt remains edible for weeks when refrigerated. The live cultures in yogurt aid digestion, boost immunity and help with lactose intolerance. Greek yogurt is a thicker, strained version.

Kefir

Another fermented milk product, kefir, uses a blend of yeast and lactic acid bacteria to ferment milk into a smooth, drinkable consistency with an effervescent zing. It can be made from various milks, like cow, goat, or coconut. Kefir contains protein, calcium, and probiotics, supporting digestive and bone health.

Sourdough Bread

Fermenting flour and water forms a starter culture that gives sourdough bread the characteristic tang and rise. Wild yeasts and bacteria feed on sugars, producing lactic and acetic acids that lend sour flavor while creating air pockets, making the bread rise. Sourdough takes longer to ferment and bake but is easily digestible.

Cheese

Fermentation transforms milk into over a thousand cheese varieties. Enzymes and bacteria convert milk components into curds and whey. The whey is drained while the curds are aged, concentrating their flavor. Microbes continue fermenting the curds, enhancing taste, texture, and nutrients. Popular varieties include cheddar, mozzarella, and Parmesan.

Wine and Beer

Wine and beer rely on yeasts fermenting fruit or grain sugars into alcohol. Grapes are fermented into wine, while barley is malted, boiled, and fermented into beer. Fermentation yields byproducts that contribute to flavors like the fruitiness in wines or hops' bitterness in beers. Adjusting yeasts and fermentation alters the end products.

Pickles

Pickling cucumbers in brine makes classic dill or sour pickles, with vinegar and spices adding flavor. Pickled cucumbers retain their crunchy texture thanks to calcium in the brine, strengthening the pectin in their cell walls. Refrigerator pickles ferment briefly before chilling stops the process, keeping them crunchy and tangy.

Unpicked green olives are too bitter to eat. Curing them in brine or lye solution removes their bitterness and preserves them. Fermented olives develop more profound, more complex flavors. Olive pickling commonly involves salt-curing and submerging them in vinegar, brine, or olive oil. This prepares them for safe long-term storage.

Condiments

Many condiments rely on fermentation or pickling. Sauces like soy sauce, tamari, fish sauce, Worcestershire, and hot sauce derive umami flavors from fermenting grains, fish, or chilies. Pickled relishes, chutneys, and vinegar-preserved mustard enliven foods with tangy accents. Fermented condiments introduce new flavors to spice up meals.

Meats

Salted, cured meats utilize salt, bacteria, and time to prevent spoilage. Dry curing dehydrates the surface of the meat to inhibit microbial growth, while smoking imparts antibacterial compounds. Sauerkraut or kimchi juice supplies the fermenting bacteria. Air-drying and cool temperatures slow the cured meats' fermentation, concentrating flavors for charcuterie like salami, prosciutto, and pepperoni.

The Health Benefits of Consuming Fermented Vegetables

Fermented veggies like sauerkraut, kimchi, and pickles have been enjoyed for ages as tasty, preserved foods. But beyond their bold, tangy flavors, these ferments can boost your health in many ways. As you learn how good fermented produce can be for you, you'll want to eat more. This section explores the awesome health perks you can get from fermented vegetables.

Gut Health

One of the most researched benefits of fermented veggies is better digestive and gut health. The live microbes in ferments give you probiotics that populate your microbiome. Regularly eating fermented foods helps create a diverse, balanced community of bacteria and yeast in your gut. This has some nice upsides:

Better Digestion and Nutrient Absorption

The microbes in ferments, like kimchi, help you break down and digest your food. Their enzymes degrade fibers, proteins, and carbs that humans can't handle alone, unlocking more nutrients and energy from your meals. The bacteria make vitamins and compounds that improve digestion and nutrient absorption. Overall, probiotics enhance your ability to get sustenance from your diet.

Immune Support

A robust microbiome acts as a first defense against pathogens by crowding them out. Good bacteria strengthen the intestinal barrier to prevent bacteria and toxins from leaking from your gut. Microbes further interact with your immune system to modulate responses. Therefore, probiotics from fermented veggies boost your natural immunity.

Reduced Inflammation

Lactic acid bacteria have anti-inflammatory effects in your gut. They lower inflammatory cytokine levels and protect against damage to your intestinal lining. Probiotics change gut bacteria to reduce inflammation. Less gut inflammation means less discomfort and better overall health.

Improved Regularity

The helpful microorganisms in fermented veggies like sauerkraut can normalize your bowel habits. Probiotics decrease gut transit time and make you poop more often if you're usually constipated. For diarrhea, they firm up stools by absorbing water and slowing motility. The microbiome modulation promotes ideal regularity.

As you can see, nourishing your microbiome with fermented veggie probiotics encourages optimal digestion, immunity, and intestinal health. The more strains of lactic acid bacteria you eat, the more diverse benefits you'll get.

Weight Management

Chowing down on fermented foods like pickles, kimchi, and kombucha may help you lose weight and keep it off by:

Appetite Control

Fermented veggies provide probiotics that influence appetite hormones like ghrelin and leptin. This makes you feel full faster and for longer. Microbes also reduce appetite by slowing digestion and absorbing nutrients over time. The bottom line is probiotics help control hunger urges.

Fat and Sugar Metabolism

Your gut microbes are essential in metabolizing fat, carbs, and protein. Probiotics from fermented veggies change your microbiome makeup to optimize digestion and calories extracted from food. They alter how you obtain energy from fat versus carbs. This metabolic programming promotes a healthy weight.

Gut Barrier Function

As mentioned, probiotics improve gut barrier integrity to prevent toxins and bacteria leakage. This lowers systemic inflammation linked to obesity and metabolic issues. A strong gut barrier ensures appetite hormones aren't disrupted.

Adding more probiotic fermented foods into your diet can support a healthy weight and metabolism. A balanced microbiome optimized by ferments helps you digest and process nutrients effectively.

Detoxification

The good bacteria in fermented veggies can help remove toxins and waste from your body in a few ways:

Heavy Metal Binding

Lactic acid bacteria like those in kimchi and sauerkraut bind with heavy metals like lead, cadmium, and arsenic in your gut. The metals are pooped out rather than absorbed into your bloodstream. Studies show fermented foods lower heavy metals in people with high exposure.

Liver Support

Microbes from fermented vegetables produce compounds like organic acids and peptides that support your liver. This allows your liver to metabolize better and eliminate toxins. Probiotics reduce liver inflammation and damage from harmful gut bacteria. Your microbiome assists your liver in detoxing.

Waste Removal

The beneficial microorganisms in ferments metabolize and facilitate the removal of byproducts, ammonia, and nitrogen compounds by your kidneys. They lower toxin production by pathogens and support overall kidney function for more efficient waste excretion.

Bringing traditionally fermented foods into your diet aids your body's natural detox systems. The probiotics in ferments like pickles bind toxins and support the organs vital for removing waste.

Improved Nutrition

Besides probiotics, fermenting also boosts the nutritional value of vegetables:

Bioavailability

Through enzymatic activity, Fermentation breaks down fibers and anti-nutrients like phytic acid in plants. This liberates nutrients like minerals, amino acids, and phenolics that would otherwise be poorly absorbed. So, fermenting makes the existing vitamins and minerals in veggies more bioavailable.

Synthesis

Microbes produce various nutrients during fermentation. Bacteria synthesize B vitamins, vitamin K2, omega-3 fatty acids, and others. Fermenting vegetables with certain bacteria purposefully increases synthesized nutrients' levels. Hence, more bioactive compounds become available.

Preservation

Fermenting preserves nutrients that would otherwise break down during cooking or spoilage. Enzymes release antioxidants from plant cell walls. Fermented veggies retain nutrients better long-term than fresh or frozen. Preserving antioxidants and delicate vitamins maximizes nutrition.

Fermented vegetables deliver extra nutritional firepower by improving nutrient bioavailability, microbial synthesis, and preservation. The live cultures transform veggies into a more concentrated and bioactive superfood.

Disease Prevention

Regularly eating fermented vegetables as part of a balanced diet can help prevent chronic conditions like:

Cancer

Probiotics modulate detoxification, inflammation, immune function, and oxidation to suppress tumor growth. Specific lactic acid bacteria strains show anti-cancer effects by inhibiting the growth and spread of human cancer cells in trials. The phytochemicals in fermented veggies add to this anticarcinogenic protection.

Cardiovascular Disease

In studies, probiotic lactic acid bacteria were shown to lower cholesterol, blood pressure, and arterial plaque buildup. They also decrease the oxidation of LDL cholesterol. Fermented veggie microbes promote heart health and reduce cardiovascular disease risk through these mechanisms.

Diabetes

Fermented foods with probiotics improve insulin sensitivity and blood sugar control. Probiotics protect pancreatic beta cell function to preserve insulin production. Microbes can alter gene expression related to diabetes development. So, including ferments in your diet could prevent and manage diabetes.

Mental Health Conditions

Your gut microbiome communicates with your brain through the gut-brain axis. Probiotics benefit mental health by reducing inflammation, producing mood-boosting neurotransmitters and metabolites, and balancing stress response. Regularly eating fermented veggies could prevent anxiety, depression, and stress.

While studies are still working out the mechanisms, the live cultures in fermented vegetables clearly support whole-body wellness. Protect your health by making them a habit.

Longevity

The wide-ranging benefits of probiotic fermented foods suggest they may promote longevity. The microbes reduce factors implicated in aging, like chronic inflammation, oxidation, glycemic response, and arterial stiffening. Through direct and indirect mechanisms, lactobacilli and other live cultures appear to prolong lifespan in animal models. Although human trials are needed, fermented veggies like sauerkraut show promise for anti-aging effects, given their health perks. Adding them to your meals could help you live longer.

Risk Reduction

For most healthy people, regularly eating fermented vegetables is safe and beneficial. But some things to consider include:

- People with compromised immunity should minimize fermented foods until their condition improves. The microbes might increase infection risk.

- Those with histamine intolerance could react to high-histamine ferments like sauerkraut, tempeh, and kombucha.

- Anyone with active gut inflammation should introduce ferments slowly to give the microbiome time to acclimate.

Otherwise, the biggest risk with ferments is overdoing high-sodium varieties if you have hypertension or kidney issues. Stick to moderate portions, and opt for low-salt options when possible.

With some basic precautions, the rewards you gain from adding fermented produce outweigh the risks. Experiment to find varieties that make you feel vibrant, energized, and healthy.

Getting Started

Here are some tips to start reaping the wellness perks of fermented veggies:

- Try small sampler amounts of different ferments to find appealing textures and flavors you enjoy. Good starter picks include dill pickle chips, cabbage kimchi, and sauerkraut.

- Look for raw, unpasteurized versions with live cultures for probiotic power. Check labels for "naturally fermented" and "contains live cultures."

- Aim for 2-4 servings of fermented veggies weekly as part of an overall healthy diet, and scale up from there. A serving is around 1/4 - 1/2 cup.

- When you're ready to DIY, start with easy beginner veggie ferments like carrots, radishes, and cucumbers before trying cauliflower or cabbage.

As you make fermented produce a regular habit, notice how your digestion, energy, and cravings respond. Let your body guide you to the optimal amount and ferment types. Getting creative with fermented condiments can make healthy eating more fun.

Chapter 2: Getting Started: Essential Tools and Ingredients

Fermenting and pickling allow you to transform fresh ingredients into tangy, flavored preserves, but they require special supplies and a few safety precautions. In this chapter, you'll learn what you need to get started.

2. Seasonings are important for fermentation. Source: https://unsplash.com/photos/a-shelf-filled-with-lots-of-different-types-of-spices-1I9bMlIAIBM?utm_content=creditShareLink&utm_medium=referral&utm_source=unsplash

First, you'll learn the ideal jars, lids, salts, and seasonings to select as a beginning pickler or fermenter. You'll get an overview of the essential equipment and ingredients.

Next, you'll discover how to choose top-quality fresh vegetables, fruits, and other produce to ensure your ferments and pickles turn out great. You'll get tips on what to look for when you go shopping.

Finally, you'll go over crucial safety guidelines. Fermenting requires careful sanitation to avoid contamination. You'll learn the best practices for maintaining a clean workspace, personal hygiene, and avoiding cross-contamination when fermenting your creations.

Following the recommendations in this chapter will set you up with the essential tools, ingredients, and food safety knowledge to confidently begin pickling and fermenting safely at home.

Introduction to Pickling Ingredients and Equipment

Here are the essential tools and components to preserve fruits and vegetables using brines, vinegar, and fermentation.

Jars and Lids

The jars and lids for pickling and fermentation are crucial. They must withstand the pickling process while keeping air out. Here are some guidelines:

- **Glass Jars** - Glass mason jars are ideal for pickling and fermenting. They won't react with brines and come in standard and wide-mouth sizes. Look for jars free of cracks or chips. Ball and Kerr are reputable Mason jar brands.

- **Plastic Jars** - For short-term fridge storage of quick pickles, food-grade plastic jars work well. But avoid using plastic long-term as the acids can interact with the plastic.

- **Jar Size** - Match the jar size to the amount of produce you pickle. For larger batches, a 1-quart wide-mouth jar is ideal. For smaller amounts, use pint jars or 8 oz. jelly jars.

- **Metal Lids** - Use new metal canning lids each time you pickle. The sealing compound degrades after one use. Lids should be free of dents or flaws.

- **Screw Bands** - These metal rings screw onto jars to hold lids in place during processing. Reusing clean screw bands is fine.

- **Airlock Lids** - These special lids allow air to escape during fermentation without allowing oxygen back in. They have a water seal or gasket mechanism you must monitor.

- **Regular Lids** - You can use new canning lids for fermentation if airlock lids are unavailable. However, avoid fully tightening them so gases can be released.

When selecting jars and lids for pickling and fermenting, always inspect them closely and use products designed for home canning. It helps keep your brined or fermented produce safe.

Salt

3. Salt is a vital pickling and fermenting ingredient. Source: https://unsplash.com/photos/brown-wooden-spoon-4OfaTz6SdYs?utm_content=creditShareLink&utm_medium=referral&utm_source=unsplash

Salt is a vital pickling and fermenting ingredient. It provides flavor while inhibiting unwanted microbial growth. Consider these salt options:

- **Kosher Salt** - Coarse kosher salt works well to draw moisture from vegetables. The larger grains make it easy to measure and distribute evenly.

- **Sea Salt** - Sea salts contain trace minerals. Their fine texture dissolves easily into brines. The mild flavor lets the ingredients shine.

- **Pickling Salt** - Fine-grained without iodine or anti-caking agents, allows the saltiness to be precisely controlled. Popular name brands are Canning & Pickling Salt and Ball Pickle Crisp.

- **Himalayan Pink Salt** - This handsome pink salt has a mild salty taste. The mineral content in this salt adds a subtle complexity. Use it for subtle flavor in ferments.

- **Curing Salt** - Containing sodium nitrite, curing salts helps prevent botulism when pickling meats. Use as directed since nitrites are toxic in high amounts.

For most vegetable pickling, kosher or pickling salts are good choices. Avoid table salt, which has additives. Weigh the salt for accuracy versus measuring volumes. Also, use non-iodized salts, as iodine can cause discoloration.

Vinegar

Adding vinegar lowers pH and imparts flavor into many pickling brines. Which type you use affects the result. Consider these vinegar options:

- **White Distilled Vinegar** - With 5% acidity, this inexpensive clear vinegar provides tartness without altering color. It's a versatile pickling vinegar.

- **Apple Cider Vinegar** - Made from fermented apples, this golden vinegar has a fruity aroma and mellow acidity at 5%. It's excellent for chutneys and brines.

- **Wine Vinegar** - White wine, red wine, and champagne vinegar range from 5-7% acidity with sophisticated fruitiness. They shine in gourmet pickles.

- **Balsamic Vinegar** - Aged balsamic is too low-acid at 6% pH for pickling alone. It's excellent blended with more acidic vinegar for flavor.

- **Rice Vinegar** - This very mild, clear vinegar made from rice only reaches 4% acidity. Combine it with stronger vinegar or use small amounts in Asian pickles.

Always use vinegar that is clearly labeled as 5% acidity for pickling. This acid level reliably prevents bacterial growth while pickling. Always ensure vinegar is marked for food use, not industrial or cleaning.

Water

The water for making brines is significant. Here are water tips for pickling:

- **Filtered Water** – Using filtered, rather than hard tap water, will create the best tasting, most translucent pickles with few mineral deposits.

- **Bottled Water** – As long as it doesn't contain carbonation, bottled drinking water can be used.

- **Boiled Tap Water** – If using unfiltered tap water, boiling it vigorously first will remove chlorine and dissolved minerals. Let it fully cool before making brine.

- **Spring or Distilled Water** – Pure water sources allow brine flavors to shine. But they lack the beneficial minerals that filtered water provides.

Avoid using hard well water or straight tap water, as sediment and off-flavors can result. Never use chemically softened water, as salts can interfere with the pickling process. Your pickles will look and taste their best with purified water.

Spices and Flavorings

Spices, herbs, and aromatics liven up ferments and pickled foods. Tailor these seasonings to suit your taste:

- **Fresh Herbs** – Flavor brines with dill, cilantro, oregano, basil, bay leaves, or thyme. Rinse and pat dry before submerging.

- **Spice Blends** – Customize spice mixes with favorites like coriander, mustard seeds, peppercorns, chilies, garlic, cinnamon sticks, or cloves.

- **Alliums** – Onions, shallots, leeks, and garlic accentuate flavors in blends or ferments.

- **Pepper Varieties** – Black, white, green, and red peppers add heat. Chili flakes bring mild warmth or sear.

- **Sweeteners** – A pinch of sugar balances the sourness in brines. Alternatives like honey, maple syrup, or agave nectar also work.

- **Citrus Zest** – Strips of oranges, lemons, or limes contribute bright, fresh, citrusy notes.

Experiment with your favorite aromatic spices, herbs, and flavorings to craft signature pickled creations.

Produce

Naturally, the ripe fruits or crisp vegetables you pickle significantly impact the finished flavors. You need to produce such as:

- Cucumber, cauliflower, onions, peppers, carrots.

- Leafy greens such as beet leaves, collard greens, kale, mustard greens, and cabbage.

- Various fruits.

Canning Tools

Specialized canning tools help make preparing produce, filling jars, and processing pickles safer and easier:

- **Food Processor** – Quickly chops vegetables uniformly with sharp blades.

- **Kitchen Scale** – Weighing salt and brine ingredients provides precise measurements.

- **Wide Mouth Funnel** – Useful for filling jars with chopped veggies and pouring in brine without spilling.

- **Bubble Releaser** – This plastic wand releases trapped air bubbles for a proper seal.

- **Canning Tongs** – Extra-long to grip jars in boiling water. Protects against burns.

- **Jar Lifter** – This heat-resistant gripper lets you securely grip and maneuver hot jars when canning.

- **Lid Wand** – Magnets on this wand make lids easy to lower onto filled jars. It keeps your hands away from hot jars.

Investing in purpose-made canning gadgets simplifies many steps for a novice pickler. Later, you can improvise with typical kitchen tools.

Fermentation Crocks and Weights

For whole or chunky vegetable ferments like sauerkraut, specialized crocks make the process easier. They have heavy ceramic weights to submerge vegetables under brine as fermentation occurs. Here's what to look for when selecting a fermenting crock:

- **Material** – Porous stoneware, glass, or food-safe plastic buckets work. Avoid reactive metals. Crocks shouldn't contain lead or toxic paints.

- **Size** – Crocks as small as 1 quart up to 1 gallon sizes are useful, depending on the batch needs. Larger is better for beginners.

- **Lid** – Crocks should have a wide opening for ingredients and water-tight lids. Some feature airlock valves to release oxygen.

- **Weight** – A ceramic disk fits inside the crock to keep vegetables forced down in the brine. It should be solid and heavy.

- **Shape** – Cylindrical pots allow better compression than straight-sided containers. Curved sides encourage brine circulation.

Quality crocks designed for fermenting make the process reliable and mess-free for novice fermenters. With practice, you can improvise weights and lids for other vessels.

pH Testing Supplies

A pH meter is extremely helpful for beginners to achieve the proper acidity for pickled and fermented foods safely.

- **pH Meter** – This specialized tool measures pH electronically with colored display lights. Look for one with automatic temperature compensation for accuracy.

- **pH Strips** – These disposable strips indicate pH with the color they turn when dipped in liquid. They offer a more affordable option but can be harder to decipher.

- **Calibration Tools** – Regularly use calibration powder or solutions to recalibrate electronic pH testers for dependable results.

- **Records** – Tracking recipe ingredients plus beginning and ending pH will help you hone better brine formulas and fermentation times.

While not mandatory, a digital pH meter takes the guesswork out of achieving safe pH levels below 4.6. It ensures your homemade creations are properly preserved against dangerous microbes.

Safety Equipment

4. *Oven mitts can minimize risks. Source: Henry Söderlund from Helsinki, Finland, CC BY 2.0 <https://creativecommons.org/licenses/by/2.0>, via Wikimedia Commons: https://commons.wikimedia.org/wiki/File:Oven_mitts_-_by_Henry_S%C3%B6derlund_(53394504077).jpg*

Take safety seriously when working with hot liquids, sterilizing jars, and handling fresh produce during pickling. These supplies minimize risks:

- **Oven Mitts and Gloves** – Protects hands from hot jars and processing pots. Use gloves when prepping peppers or other irritants.

- **Apron** – Keeps clothes protected from stains when filling and handling dripping jars. Look for aprons with useful pockets.

- **Eye Protection** – Vinegar fumes, steaming pots, and bubbling brines can burn eyes. Wear shatterproof safety goggles.

- **Vinegar-Safe Surfaces** – Avoid stainless steel, iron, or enamel pans. Reactive to vinegar, they create off-flavors and unhealthy metal contamination.

- **Non-Slip Mats** – These grippy pads provide traction to prevent falls when working on wet surfaces around sinks and stoves.

- **First Aid Kit** – Keep bandages, antibiotic cream, and burn gel nearby to treat minor cuts or scalds.

With a safe setup and practices, you can avoid accidents and be assured your food is contamination-free. Foresight and preparedness are essential when undertaking fermenting or pickling projects.

Refrigeration Equipment

Once sufficiently fermented or pickled, produce needs rapid chilling and cold storage to halt fermentation and retain freshness long-term. Here's helpful refrigeration gear:

- **Refrigerator Thermometer** – Monitor that your fridge maintains 40°F or below. Fermented veggies require consistent cold temperatures.

- **Freezer Thermometer** – Ensure your freezer stays at 0°F to allow long-term freezer storage.

- **Cooler** – A plug-in drink cooler lets you chill jars rapidly after heat processing. Quick cooling prevents over-fermenting.

- **Refrigerator Space** – Make room to store filled jars and fermentation vessels. Keep them on interior shelves, not on the door.

- **Freezer Space** – Leave room for sliced fruits and frozen produce you'll use for pickling. Organize jars for easy identification.

Proper refrigeration and freezing preserves crisp textures and stops fermentation at your ideal tanginess. Maximize these appliances' cool storage capabilities when pickling in quantity.

The right ingredients, equipment, and refrigeration are critical to pickling and fermenting success. Use this overview of essential canning and fermenting supplies to equip your kitchen with everything to safely transform seasonal produce into delicious pickled creations. With quality tools and components, you will set yourself up for tasty results and enjoyable DIY food preservation.

Selecting Quality Vegetables and Additional Ingredients

Choosing excellent quality vegetables and additional ingredients is essential for creating delicious and safely preserved pickles, chutneys, ferments, and more. The freshness and characteristics of the main components significantly influence the results. This chapter provides tips to help you select top produce and complementary ingredients.

Picking Peak Produce

When shopping for veggies to pickle or ferment, follow these general guidelines:

- **Seek Out Local, in-Season Produce.** Fruits and vegetables from nearby farms will be garden-fresh. Their peak ripeness offers the best texture and flavor.

- **Look for Vibrant, Robust Colors.** Depending on the type, the produce should be richly hued without blemishes. Avoid produce with mold, shriveling, or dark spots.

- **Examine Their Structure and Firmness.** Depending on the vegetable or fruit, it should feel heavy, crisp, and free of soft spots that indicate spoilage.

- **Sniff the Aromas**. The produce should smell fresh, with no off odors. Trust your nose to detect issues.

- **Feel the Weight**. Heavier vegetables and fruits are more hydrated and ripe. Lightness can mean dryness and age.

- **Ask Questions**. If you are uncertain about an item's freshness, ask staff for the harvesting date, shelf-life, and storage tips.

With practice, you'll learn to identify peak produce ready for pickling and fermenting by looking, feeling, and smelling. Farmers markets offer ripe, local bounty.

Selecting Cucumbers

Since cucumbers are the basis of popular pickles, pay extra attention when purchasing them:

- **Choose Smaller Varieties.** The bumpy, thin-skinned Kirby or Persian cucumbers offer the best texture and flavor for whole pickles.

- **Seek Uniform Sizing, about 4 to 6 Inches, for Easy Packing into Jars**. Avoid oddly shaped or extremely large cucumbers.

- **Look for Deep Green Skins Free of Blemishes or Yellowing.** Brown spots and dull colors indicate age.

- **Heft Cucumbers to Check for Heaviness and Firmness.** Pass on withered or mushy ends.

- **Smell for Fresh, Bright Aromas**. Avoid cucumbers with off smells suggesting mold and spoilage.

- **For Unwaxed Fruits, Check the Label or Ask Vendors.** The wax coating must be scrubbed off before pickling.

Start with premium pickling cucumber varieties harvested at peak ripeness. This gives finished pickles pleasing uniformity and crunch.

Choosing Cabbage for Kraut and Kimchi

When selecting cabbage heads for sauerkraut, kimchi, and other ferments, look for:

- Compact, heavy heads that feel dense and substantial in your hands, a sign of high internal moisture.

- Avoid cabbage with loose outer leaves or splits exposing interior leaves. This indicates drying.

- Look for crisp, brightly-hued leaves without spots or yellowing. Brown edges show oxidation.

- Cabbage should smell fresh, akin to the scent of a freshly mown lawn. Pass on musty odors.

- Choose greener napa or savoy cabbage varieties over pale green heads for kimchi and coleslaws.

- For sauerkraut, green or purple cabbage works well. Avoid large, firm heads that can be fibrous.

The suitable cabbage provides ample fluid and fermentable sugars for successful DIY kraut or kimchi.

Picking Produce for Pickled Mixes

When selecting vegetables and fruits for combinations like relishes, giardiniera, or chutneys, follow similar freshness guidelines:

- Seek out produce nearing ripeness but not overripe and soft. This ensures ideal texture.

- Look for vibrant colors without blemishes, bruises, or moldy spots. Smaller uniform sizes can also be appealing.

- Avoid overly dry or shriveled fruits and vegetables. Some surface wrinkling might be expected.

- Give a gentle squeeze to check for ideal firmness and turgor. Pass on excessively soft or mushy spots.

- Rely on scent. Avoid off aromas like fermentation or rot setting in.

- With greens like kale or peppers, pass on sliminess or dark water-soaked appearance.

A diversity of fresh, just-ripening produce will pickle into a flavorful and visually appealing medley.

Choosing Vegetables for Fermentation

Follow similar advice when selecting vegetables destined for ferments like kimchi, curtido, sauerkraut, or other cultured vegetables:

- **Select Young, Tender Vegetables.** Avoid larger, more mature specimens that may be fibrous.

- **Seek Out Blemish-Free, Optimally Ripe Produce with Robust Color.** Overripe veggies ferment poorly.

- **Look for Crispness and Turgor, Not a Soft or Dry Texture.** Wilting indicates loss of the moisture needed for brining.

- **Trust Your Nose to Detect Spoilage.** Avoid musty, moldy, or yeasty aromas.

- **Smaller, Uniform Sizes Allow More Efficient Fermenting.** Cut or shred larger pieces to the right size.

- For ferments featuring multiple vegetables, like curtido, choose ingredients that ripen concurrently.

Top-quality vegetables with high internal moisture will ferment vigorously and develop full flavors with pleasing texture.

Picking Fruits for Fermentation

Many fruits also ferment well into tasty products like kombucha, fruit leathers, or preserves. For these, opt for:

- Tree-ripened or vine-ripened fruits at their sweetest prime. Farm stands offer ideal picks.

- Fragrance is important. Seek out fruity aromas, not fermenting ones.

- Avoid bruised, damaged, or punctured skin. This invites unwanted microbes.

- For soft fruits like berries, refrigerate quickly. Use the same day if possible.

- With hard fruits, select those heavy for their size and free of brown spots.

- Taste samples if allowed. Tartness indicates optimal ripeness for fermenting.

Premium quality tree fruits like apples, stone fruits, or citrus provide the sugars and flavors to create outstanding fermented products.

Finding Quality Meat and Fish

Fermenting or pickling meats and fish requires sourcing the very freshest:

- Only use freshly slaughtered meat from a known, trusted source for raw cured meats.

- Seek out sushi-grade fish caught the same day for pickling. It must be impeccably fresh.

- The item should have no off odors whatsoever. Rely on your nose to detect spoiled meat or fish.

- Visually examine for the ideal red color in beef and lamb and clean white flesh in poultry or fish.

- For ground meats, ensure no brown or gray smears, indicating oxidation. The redness should be uniform.

- Ask the seller for details on the harvesting date, transport, and storage temperatures.

- Keep meats well chilled until use. Use raw cured products within the advised time frames.

Top-tier freshness is mandatory with animal proteins to prevent dangerous pathogenic bacteria.

Selecting Quality Salts

When purchasing salts for pickling brines and ferments, check for:

- Pickling or canning salts without iodine or anti-caking agents. These dissolve most reliably.

- Pure granulated white sugar without additives, bleaching, or molasses.

- Fine-grained sea or kosher salt for even distribution on produce. Coarse salt is best for fermentation brining.

- Himalayan or smoked salts for their color and subtle mineral flavors.

- Curing salts containing nitrites to prevent botulism in meat curing. Use as directed.

- Ensure salts don't contain problematic additives and are marked food grade rather than pool salts. Weigh salt quantities for the best accuracy.

Finding Good Water

The quality of your water greatly impacts pickling and fermenting outcomes. Look for:

- Bottled spring or filtered tap water for chlorine removal and a neutral taste.

- Water free of off-tastes and aromas like sulfur, chlorine, or minerals.

- Clear water without cloudiness or particles that could indicate contamination.

- If using well water, have it periodically tested for safety. Boil if uncertain.

- For fermentation requiring extra minerals, add a pinch of sea salt.

It's worth purchasing distilled, filtered, or natural spring water to start your brines and ferments with optimal taste and clarity.

Procuring Quality Vinegar

When buying vinegar for pickling, verify:

- The vinegar is marketed for food preparation rather than industrial use.

- There are no cloudy sediments or strange aromas that could indicate contamination or spoilage.

- Apple cider, white wine, and champagne vinegar offer pleasant flavor complexity.

- Balsamic adds rich flavor when blended with more acidic kinds of vinegar.

Avoid cheap distilled white vinegar, as its harsh acidity overpowers foods. With quality vinegar, just a splash brightly enhances flavors.

Finding Fresh, Fragrant Spices and Herbs

Don't underestimate the importance of fresh, robust spices and herbs for flavoring brines and ferments. Look for:

- Bright, pronounced aromas from whole dried spices like peppercorns, cloves, dill seed, and coriander.

- Vivid color and sheen on dried chilies, garlic flakes, and onion flakes.

- Crisp, green, unblemished leaves on fresh herb bunches. Avoid yellowing or wilting.

- Plump, juicy garlic bulbs free of green sprouting or moisture loss.

- Spice sets that are sold in light-protective tins to prevent UV deterioration.

- Smaller quantities of whole spices must be used within 3-6 months before losing potency.

Vibrant, fragrant spices encourage fermentation and make the flavors pop. Blend your signature mixes to add unique personality to your pickled creations.

Essential Safety Guidelines for Fermentation

Fermenting vegetables, condiments, and other foods can seem daunting at first. However, an awareness of potential risks and following key safety practices ensures your DIY ferments are delicious and healthy to enjoy. This chapter outlines fundamental guidelines for you as a beginner fermenter to avoid problems and achieve safe, high-quality results.

Sanitizing Equipment

Thoroughly cleaning and sanitizing all equipment that touches ingredients is essential to avoid dangerous microbial contamination. Here are effective sanitizing tips:

1. First, wash the jars, lids, fermenting vessels, knives, grates, and tools in hot soapy water to remove debris

and grease. Use a bottle brush to scrub inside narrow jars.

2. Rinse all items well after soaping to eliminate residues. Repeat washing if needed to eliminate clinging particles.

3. Sanitize using boiling water, steam, bleach solution, or vinegar. Boil glass jars in water for 10 minutes. Hold tools over steaming pots for a few minutes.

4. Soak washed items 1-2 minutes in a mild bleach solution of 1 teaspoon of unscented bleach per quart of cool water. Rinse extremely thoroughly after soaking to prevent residual bleach taste.

5. Use undiluted white distilled vinegar to sanitize surfaces. Spray it on and let it sit for 2-3 minutes before wiping or rinsing. It effectively kills bacteria and mold.

6. Air dry sanitized containers and equipment on dish racks or clean towels. Avoid drying with towels that can reintroduce microbes.

You remove potential contaminants with clean, sanitized gear, providing a blank slate for the desired fermentation cultures.

Avoiding Cross-Contamination

In addition to sanitizing, you must prevent cross-contamination between ingredients. Follow these tips:

- Designate certain equipment like knives, cutting boards, pans, and storage containers specifically for handling fermenting foods only. Keep these separate from other kitchen gear.

- Use separate cooler bags, storage bins, and lids for transporting produce and finished ferments. Never reuse containers that hold raw meats.

- Thoroughly scrub hands, nails, and surfaces between handling different raw ingredients like meats versus vegetables. Avoid direct contact.

- Never place fermenting vegetables or brine in contact with unwashed hands, counters, or tools. Always use sanitized jars and equipment.

- Always use a clean spoon each time when tasting fermenting foods. Never double-dip tongs, spoons, or fingers into fermenting vessels.

- Isolate fermenting foods from other items in your refrigerator's crisper drawers. Ensure they can't leak brine onto neighboring foods.

With diligence against cross-contamination from harvest to storage, you guard against foodborne illnesses, off-flavors, and poor results.

Avoiding Mold Contamination

Active mold growth can ruin a batch of fermenting vegetables. Here are tips to prevent mold:

- Always keep vegetables fully submerged under the brine. Use weights as needed so that there are no exposed pieces. Oxygen exposure encourages mold.

- Check batches daily and skim off mold filaments or white film that appear on the brine surface using a clean spoon. Then, wash the spoon thoroughly.

- Discard the entire batch if soft, colorful mold forms inside the fermenting jar. Do not attempt to scoop it out. Mold can penetrate the brine.

- Wipe the rims of jars carefully before closing the lids to remove clinging debris that could harbor mold spores. Avoid splashing brine onto lid rims.

- Use airlock-style fermenting lids to protect against oxygen entering after CO_2 release. Or loosely seal regular lids so gases can vent.

- Keep fermenting vessels in a cool area away from sunlight. Darkness and cooler temperatures inhibit mold growth.

With meticulous avoidance of oxygen exposure and prompt removal of growths, you can keep mold from gaining a foothold and ruining batches.

Preventing Kahm Yeast Formation

Along with mold, Kahm yeast is another potential fermenting contaminant requiring preventive action:

Kahm yeast forms powdery or filmy white layers on top of brine during fermentation. It's generally harmless but can impart off flavors.

- To discourage Kahm yeast, submerge vegetables fully under the brine to keep them away from oxygen. Weigh them down as needed.

- Use fresher, tightly sealed spices. Older spices can harbor wild yeast spores, leading to Kahm yeast growth.

- Stir the brine gently daily to prevent Kahm yeast from establishing on the surface. Remove any film that's present.

- If you ignore it, Kahm yeast may form tan or orange patches with fruity, yeasty aromas. Discard ferments showing these colors.

- Sanitize equipment after each use to eliminate contamination sources. Kahm yeast comes from outside environments.

Avoiding Kahm yeast requires controlling oxygen exposure, using fresh ingredients, and vigilant surface skimming during fermentation.

Ensuring Proper Brine Salinity

Getting brine salinity right is vital for safety and quality:

- Use the correct proportions of salt to water specified in recipes. Weigh salt rather than measuring by volume for accuracy.

- High salinity prevents pathogenic bacterial growth, but too much salt can inhibit desired lactic acid bacteria and enzymatic transformations.

- Low salinity risks dangerous microbes taking hold. But too little salt won't reliably discourage yeasts and mold.

- For salt ferments like sauerkraut, vigorously massage salt into vegetable leaves to leach juices that will form the brine.

- When using brine, mix it thoroughly so the salt dissolves completely before pouring it over vegetables. Stir periodically to redistribute it.

- Use cheesecloth bags or mesh strainers to separate floating spice solids from the surrounding brine.

- Check that salt concentrations stay stable as fermentation progresses. Add more brine or salt if vegetables become exposed.

By carefully calibrating salinity at safe levels, you prevent pathogenic risks and textural issues from improper saltiness.

Maintaining Anaerobic Conditions

Excluding oxygen is essential for successful anaerobic lactic acid ferments. Use these tips to maintain anaerobic conditions:

- Keep vegetables submerged beneath the brine at all times using weights as needed. Oxygen exposure halts fermentation.

- Choose vessels that minimize airspace above the brine. As CO_2 is released, it prevents oxygen from re-entering.

- Use airlock lids that allow gas release without air intake. If using regular lids, loosen them daily to "burp" ferments.

- During processing, pour brine into jars while it's still hot to displace oxygen. Leave minimal headspace before sealing.

- Once the desired fermentation is achieved, bottling in smaller containers minimizes air exposure during storage.

The goal is to curb oxygen contact before and after fermenting. Allowing air entry stalls the process and introduces potential spoilage.

Controlling Fermentation Temperature

The ambient temperature impacts fermentation speed, quality, and safety:

- Ideal temperatures for lactic acid vegetable fermentation range between 65°F - 75°F. Enzymatic reactions work best in this zone.

- Above 80°F, fermentation may happen too quickly. Textures suffer, and undesirable bacteria can proliferate. Slow it by chilling containers.

- Below 60°F, fermentation occurs very slowly or stalls entirely. Gentle warming by a few degrees nudges it along.

- Monitor room or chamber temperatures where you ferment foods. Move vessels to warmer or cooler spots as needed to maintain ideal conditions.

- Seasonal temperature fluctuations will alter ferments. In summer's heat, batches may be ready in 3-4 days versus 1-2 weeks in winter's chill.

- Adapt recipes and processes based on ambient temperatures for success. Fermenting outdoors or underground can help stabilize temperature.

Your beneficial fermentation cultures will thrive with the proper, consistent temperature range while undesirable bacteria are suppressed.

Regulating Fermentation Duration

Judging optimum fermentation length takes experience. Here are tips for fermenting safely:

- Follow recipe timelines as a starting point. The suggested durations account for proper acid development.

- Test batches regularly by tasting samples from the jar. Note flavors and aroma as fermentation progresses.

- End fermentation when the sourness, tang, and fragrance are ideal for your preferences.

- Use pH strips or meters to track acid development. Stop fermenting below pH 4.6 to prevent botulism risks.

- You can pause fermentation by chilling containers once the desired acidity forms. Refrigeration inhibits enzyme activity.

- Prolonged fermentation for months may impart overly soft textures and strong acid bite. Err on the side of shorter times.

With observation and testing, you'll learn to identify the peak stage to stop the fermentation and preserve flavors.

Handling Contaminated Ferments

If, despite precautions, a batch shows mold, yeast, ropiness, strange odors or colors, or unsafe pH:

- Never taste or eat contaminated ferments. Potential pathogens require proper disposal.

- Wear gloves when handling ruined ferments. Mold spores and bacteria can stick to surfaces and hands.

- Place unsalvageable ferments into sealed garbage bags. Tie them securely before putting them in outdoor bins.

- Scrub and sanitize jars, lids, tools, and surfaces exposed to contamination to destroy problematic microbes.

- Examine procedures to identify factors that could have allowed contamination and investigate how to improve them.

- Document ingredients and steps leading to failed batches to help pinpoint likely causes and avoid repeating issues.

With caution, learning from setbacks, and refining techniques, your skills will strengthen for crafting reliably safe, delicious homemade ferments.

Selecting Reliable Recipes

To start right, choose fermenting recipes wisely:

- Seek recipes from reputable cookbooks, university extension guides, and scientific sources to ensure safety.

- Observe proper ratios of ingredients, salt concentrations, acidity levels, and fermenting durations in recipes to prevent risks.

- Adapt recipes cautiously. Improvising too freely when learning can compromise outcomes. Stick closer to what's written.

- Avoid untested recipes that seem questionable or leave out key details on concentrations, pH, and processing steps.

- Check for well-explained scientific foundations and specific instruction versus vague outlines when using internet sources.

- Compare similar recipes to identify common recommended ingredients, fermenting times, processes, and safety measures.

Vetted recipes will set you up for fermenting accomplishment and enjoyment. As experience grows, you can later modify recipes more freely.

Preventing Contact with Reactive Surfaces

During fermenting, avoid equipment surfaces that can react with acids, imparting off-flavors of metal or chemicals:

- Use only glass, food-grade plastic, or enamelware containers. Never use reactive metals for fermenting or storage.

- Stainless steel preparation tables or pots are fine. But avoid galvanized, aluminum, copper, cast iron, or carbon steel surfaces.

- Don't use ceramic glazed crocks with crackled uneven glazes that can leach lead. Opt for plain ceramic or stoneware.

- Wooden cutting boards, paddles, and fermenting lids are ideal non-reactive choices. Use hard maple, not pine.

- For weighing brine ingredients, choose plastic or stainless steel. Metal exposed to salt and acids corrodes.

Your aim is to minimize metallic, chemical, and acidic reactions undermining safety. Non-reactive gear improves purity and flavor.

Practicing Diligent Hand Hygiene

Because fermenting relies on manual preparation, sanitary practices are imperative:

- Thoroughly wash hands in hot, soapy water before and after handling ingredients. Scrub well under nails.

- Avoid working with ingredients if you or others involved have illnesses or infections. Wait until you are fully recovered.

- Do not allow coughing, sneezing, or nose touching over fermenting foods and containers. Keep hair tied back.

- Use gloves or tongs for handling hot jars. Have clean clothes and aprons to prevent cross-contamination.

- Rinse produce well before fermenting. Scrub the skin of fruits and vegetables that will not be peeled.

- Keep pets and pests away from fermenting workspace areas. Their dander and droppings can contaminate.

With cleanliness during preparation and process monitoring, you avoid introducing unwanted bacteria that could spoil products or cause sickness.

Bottling and Storing Ferments Safely

Once Fermented:

- Transfer contents to sterilized glass jars or bottles with tight-fitting lids, ensuring no surface mold is present.

- Top up containers with fresh brine, leaving minimal airspace before sealing if needed. A pinch of citric acid helps with stabilization.

- Clean jar rims well before affixing lids. Store bottled ferments in the refrigerator or cold cellar at or below 40 °F to halt fermentation.

- Consume refrigerated vegetables within 6-8 months for best quality before losing crispness and nutrients.

- For long-term pantry storage at room temperature, follow canning procedures to seal pickled products for proper acidity.

- Freezing stops fermentation for items like kimchi. Thaw frozen ferments in the fridge before consuming within 4-6 months.

- The bounty of your fermenting efforts can provide probiotic nutrition all year long with safe bottling.

By keeping the risks of fermenting in perspective and rigorously applying basic food safety practices, your homemade creations can be delicious and healthy to enjoy. Follow trusted recipes, sanitize gear, exclude oxygen, control time and temperature, and handle ferments hygienically. Then, embrace fermentation as a satisfying hobby, yielding nutritious foods.

Chapter 3: Basic Fermentation Techniques

Fermentation relies on simple techniques that harness natural processes for preserving and enhancing foods. In this chapter, you'll learn fundamental fermentation methods to create fermented foods at home. First, you'll discover the science behind fermentation to understand the microbial activities and environmental conditions that make it happen.

5.   There are many methods for fermentation. Source: https://unsplash.com/photos/red-liquid-in-clear-glass-jar-y3idlWJFFZI?utm_content=creditShareLink&utm_medium=referral&utm_source=unsplash

Next is a step-by-step guide to vegetable lacto-fermentation so you can make sauerkraut, pickles, and other tasty, fermented veggies. Lastly, the chapter shares easy, beginner pickling recipes for quick refrigerator pickles, relishes, and fermented hot sauces you can experiment with. Mastering these fermentation techniques provides the core knowledge and skills to safely transform fresh ingredients into delicious, preserved foods with boosted nutrition and dynamic flavors.

Understanding the Science behind Fermentation

Fermentation relies on natural microbiological and chemical processes to transform and preserve foods. Grasping the science of fermentation will help you skillfully make fermented foods. This overview explains essential scientific ideas so you can understand what happens during fermentation.

Lactic Acid Bacteria

Fermentation depends on lactic acid bacteria (LAB) to effect the changes that preserve foods and create new flavors. Lactic acid bacteria are a group of gram-positive anaerobic bacteria converting sugars into cellular energy and lactic acid as a byproduct. Typical LAB in food fermentation include Lactobacillus, Leuconostoc, Pediococcus, and Streptococcus.

These bacteria live naturally on the surfaces of vegetables and fruits. The salt and temperature conditions during fermentation encourage them to grow. As LAB metabolizes sugars into lactic acid, the increasing acidity lowers pH, stopping spoilage microorganisms. LAB makes antimicrobial substances like hydrogen peroxide and bacteriocins that hinder undesirable bacteria.

Fermented vegetable products use Leuconostoc, Lactobacillus, and Pediococcus species that thrive on produce. Fermented dairy products use Streptococcus and Lactobacillus species suited to digesting lactose. Understanding the role of lactic acid bacteria is vital for succeeding at fermentation. You'll learn to create optimal conditions for the growth of good LAB.

Yeasts in Fermentation

Along with bacteria, yeasts are crucial in many fermented foods. Yeasts are eukaryotic fungi that metabolize sugars into ethanol and carbon dioxide. Saccharomyces is the most common yeast genus in food fermentation, which efficiently converts sugar into CO_2 and alcohol. Beer, wine, bread, and vinegar rely on yeast fermentation. The byproducts like CO_2, alcohol, and acidic compounds add flavor, leavening, and preservative qualities.

Yeasts need anaerobic conditions, 25–30°C temperatures, and enough sugars. How much yeast you add impacts fermentation speed. Some fermented foods, like kombucha, have symbiotic cultures of yeast and bacteria, making a unique blend of microbial metabolites. While undesirable in vegetable ferments, yeast's contributions are effective in fermented drinks, baked goods, and vinegar. Using the right yeast strains and fermentation conditions lets you make a variety of yeast-fermented foods and drinks.

Enzymatic Reactions

Like microbes, enzymes naturally present in plants are essential in fermentation. Enzymes in vegetables, fruits, milk, and grains help break down complex carbohydrates, proteins, and fats while fermenting. For instance, proteases break down proteins into amino acids, while amylases convert starches into simple sugars for microbes to digest. Cellulases degrade plant cell walls, contributing to softening in fermented veggies like pickles.

Enzymatic activity decreases over time but continues for weeks in anaerobic fermentation. Low temperatures and high salt slow enzymatic reactions, while higher temperatures within specific ranges speed them up. Enzymatic changes complement microbial activity, enhancing flavors, textures, and nutrient availability. While less significant than microbes, enzymes facilitate important changes in fermenting foods.

Sugars Fueling Fermentation

Fermentation needs sugars to feed the microbes and yeasts doing the transformations. LAB, yeasts, and enzymes require carbohydrates for food. The main sugar sources are fructose, glucose, and sucrose. Starches in foods like grains and some veggies are converted into fermentable sugars by amylase enzymes. The milk sugar lactose provides the carbohydrate substrate for fermentation in dairy products.

Fruits offer much sucrose, glucose, and fructose to support yeasts that turn sugar into alcohol in wine and cider. The amount of fermentable sugars influences the degree of acidity and CO_2 or alcohol produced. Adding sugars can be necessary to support fermentation in certain low-sugar vegetables fully. Providing enough fermentable sugars allows LAB, yeasts, and enzymes to prosper and change the food.

Lactic Acid in Preservation

A significant goal of vegetable fermentation using LAB is preservation through acidification; as LAB metabolizes sugars into lactic acid, acidity rises, lowering the food's pH. Lactic acid splits into lactate and hydrogen ions. More H+ ions mean lower pH. Increasing acidity eventually passes the pH level to prevent pathogen growth, such as Clostridium botulinum bacteria. A pH at or below 4.6 stops C. botulinum, making fermented vegetables shelf-stable when canned properly.

Besides lowering pH, lactic acid has antimicrobial properties, extending shelf life. The flavor from lactic acid provides a tangy taste in fermented vegetables. Too much acidity is overly sharp. Hence, reaching the right acidity through lactic acid fermentation is vital for the safety and taste of preserved fermented vegetables.

Salt's Multifaceted Roles

Salt affects fermentation in several significant ways. Salt lowers water activity, stopping unwanted microbial growth. High salinity encourages good lactic bacteria species to grow. Salt ions interrupt cellular processes that spoilage microbes need. Salt raises osmotic pressure, pulling water from plant cells. This firms texture but also provides the moisture LAB needs to grow.

Salt slows enzymes like those converting starches and softening vegetables. It balances flavor while keeping a crunchy texture. Salt starts lactic acid bacteria fermentation on cabbage leaves as juices get pulled out. In brined pickles, salt maintains a crisp texture while allowing fermentation. The proper salt concentrations promote good fermentation while suppressing harmful microbes and enzymes. Mastering salt's varied impacts gives you leverage to guide fermentation and get the perfect results.

The Anaerobic Advantage

Excluding oxygen is vital for effective fermentation. Lactic acid bacteria and many yeasts thrive without oxygen, so aerobic molds and spoilers cannot survive. Submerging foods under liquid keeps oxygen out. Weights keep vegetables immersed while fermenting. CO_2 produced during fermentation gets trapped in jars, blocking oxygen from re-entering.

Airlock lids allow gas release while preventing oxygen. Regular lids can be loosened to "burp" escaping gases. Once anaerobic conditions form, facultative LAB shift metabolism to work best sans oxygen. Anaerobic conditions enable key enzymatic fermentation that oxygen would halt. Understanding anaerobiosis lets you maximize fermentation while avoiding spoilage.

Temperature Effects on Fermentation

Temperature impacts fermentation speed and active microbes. Different bacteria and yeasts in fermentation thrive in varying temperature ranges. Cooler temperatures below 50°F slow fermentation. Warmer temperatures between 60-85°F speed it up. Ideal fruit and vegetable lactic acid fermentation is between 64-72°F since LAB likes slight warmth.

At higher temperatures, enzymatic reactions accelerate rapidly. Unwanted proteolysis can cause bitterness. Above 85°F, LAB struggles while spoilers proliferate. Refrigerating fermented foods stops microbial and enzymatic activity, essentially pausing the process. By controlling ambient temperature, you can achieve the perfect conditions for the fermenting microbes.

Additional Chemical Transformations

Alongside microbes, fermentation enables useful chemical reactions. Acidic conditions break down antinutrients, like phytic acid, freeing up minerals to absorb better. Proteins get broken into amino acids, and fats split into fatty acids, making nutrients more bioavailable. Vitamin levels increase through microbial metabolite synthesis. For instance, sauerkraut has more vitamin C than raw cabbage.

Flavors change as triglycerides undergo enzymatic hydrolysis, generating free fatty acids that heighten taste. With prolonged aging over months or years, complex aromas develop from reactions between carbohydrates, amino acids, and fatty acids. Antioxidants are synthesized, upping the health benefits of traditionally fermented foods. Besides shaping texture and taste, fermentation improves nutritional value through diverse chemical changes.

While you don't need to master microbiology, grasping fermentation's basic science helps you safely guide the process and consistently achieve your intended results. Avoiding problems and encouraging optimal conditions lets you reap delicious, nutritious rewards from homemade ferments.

Step-by-Step Guide to Lacto-Fermentation

Lacto-fermentation is preserving vegetables and other foods by fermenting them with lactic acid bacteria. This ancient method of food preservation produces tangy, probiotic-rich foods excellent for gut health.

Lacto-fermented foods add a tangy, savory, umami flavor to meals. Their unique sour taste wakes up bland dishes, providing a healthy alternative to salt for adding flavor. Adding more lacto-fermented foods to your diet offers an array of nutritional and health upsides.

Overview of the Lacto-Fermentation Process

The magic of lacto-fermentation relies on natural fermentation that occurs when lactic acid bacteria (LAB) feed on the sugars and starch in vegetables. Here is an overview.

Vegetables are submerged in a brine solution of water and salt. The salt helps draw water out of the vegetables via osmosis. The vegetables' natural bacteria rapidly multiply, feeding on their inherent sugars and starches. This fermentative activity converts the sugars into lactic acid, acetic acid, and small amounts of alcohol. The organic acids produced drop the pH level of the vegetables, making the environment too acidic for dangerous microorganisms like botulism-causing bacteria to grow and thrive. However, the beneficial LAB bacteria thrive in this acidic anaerobic environment.

Given the right conditions, the LAB ferments the vegetables for days or weeks. This extended fermentation time preserves the vegetables for several months without canning or freezing. The result is a tangy, probiotic, and enzyme-rich lacto-fermented food, adding flavor, complexity, and nutrition to meals. Sauerkraut, pickles, kimchi, kvass, and other traditional lacto-fermented foods rely on this transformative process.

While microbial activity drives this fascinating fermentative process, you can guide and control fermentation by submerging vegetables, maintaining the proper temperature, and allowing gases to vent from the fermentation vessel.

Equipment and Supplies for Lacto-Fermentation

Lacto-fermenting vegetables at home does not require specialized equipment. You likely already have most, if not all, of the supplies in your kitchen. Here is what you need:

- **Mason Jars** - You will ferment chopped or grated vegetables in a 1-quart or 2-quart wide-mouth mason jar. The wide openings make adding vegetables and pressing them down to remove air pockets easy. Use a new lid each time you start a new fermented vegetable batch.

- **Lids** - Rather than tightly screwing on jar lids, cover the fermenting jars with a permeable fabric like cheesecloth or muslin secured with a rubber band or string. This allows carbon dioxide and other gases produced during fermentation to vent while keeping dust and insects out.

- **Canning Funnel and Jar Lifter** - A wide-mouth funnel simplifies guiding vegetables neatly into the jar. Jar lifters let you grip jars tightly from the top when jostling them to pack in vegetables.

- **Vegetables** - Nearly any vegetable can be lacto-fermented, including cabbage, carrots, beets, onions, garlic, green beans, cauliflower, and many more. Cabbage is the most frequent choice.

- **Water and Salt** - You make a brine with non-chlorinated water and add unrefined sea salt or pickling salt, which doesn't contain anti-caking agents that can cause cloudiness. Plain table salt also works.

- **Herbs, Spices, Garlic** - You can add layers of fresh or dried herbs, spices, garlic, hot peppers, etc., to suit your taste. Some classic choices are dill, caraway seeds, bay leaves, mustard seeds, and coriander. Experiment to find your favorites.

- **Jar Weights** - Weights placed on top of the vegetables help keep them fully submerged under the brine as gases form and cause vegetables to rise. You can purchase glass fermentation weights or use a smaller jelly jar filled with water inside the main fermenting jar.

- **Kitchen Scale** - A digital kitchen scale lets you accurately weigh vegetables and salt to achieve the proper ratios for successful fermentation.

Choosing Vegetables and Spices for Fermentation

6. *Almost any edible vegetable can be lacto-fermented. Source: https://unsplash.com/photos/a-pile-of-different-types-of-vegetables-on-a-white-surface-5aJVJvJ9rG8?utm_content=creditShareLink&utm_medium=referral&utm_source=unsplash*

You can lacto-ferment nearly any edible vegetable. Some top choices include:

- **Cabbage** - The most popular choice, green or red cabbage, makes classic tangy sauerkraut.

- **Carrots** - Great alone or combined with cabbage. They provide a pop of color.

- **Beets** - Vibrantly hued beets become a beautiful salad topper or side dish once fermented.

- **Onions** - Their sharp bite mellows nicely during fermentation.

- **Garlic** - The flavors of whole or minced garlic cloves become more pronounced.

- **Green beans** - They retain their signature crunch when fermented.

- **Radishes** - The spicy kick of radishes pairs well with milder veggies.

- **Turnips** - Pungent, hearty turnips complement cabbage family vegetables.

- **Cauliflower or broccoli** - Use the raw florets or chopped pieces for a probiotic-rich veggie side.

You can experiment with fermenting asparagus, Brussels sprouts, bell peppers, pumpkin, and almost any produce you enjoy. Select the freshest produce possible, choosing vegetables without mushy spots or mold. Briefly rinse vegetables under cool water, but don't soak them before fermenting. Start with cabbage or carrots for your first batches, which ferment easily and quickly.

Add aromatics like spices, herbs, garlic, chilies, etc., for more complex flavors. Some examples are caraway seeds, bay leaves, mustard seeds, dill, coriander seeds, jalapeno, or peppers, and play around with your preferred spice combinations.

Step-by-Step Instructions for Basic Lacto-Fermented Vegetables

Follow these straightforward steps for making your first mason jars of tasty lacto-fermented vegetables:

1. Gather your vegetables, spices, and fermentation equipment. You need 1 to 2 pounds of vegetables per 1 quart fermentation jar.

2. Rinse your chosen vegetables briefly under cold running water. Trim off old, mushy, or molded spots. Peel the vegetables if desired.

3. Prep the vegetables by grating, shredding, finely chopping, or slicing them into small pieces. Cutting them smaller increases the surface area and speeds up fermentation.

4. Place the prepped vegetables into a large bowl. Add preferred spices, herbs, garlic, or other seasonings. Mix everything well with clean hands.

5. Weigh your bowl filled with the mixed seasoned vegetables. For each pound of vegetables, you need 2 tablespoons of salt. Use your digital kitchen scale to calculate the precise salt amount required.

6. Combine the measured salt with 4 cups of non-chlorinated water in a separate container. Stir continuously until the salt fully dissolves to make the brine.

7. Place your wide-mouth funnel snugly in the jar opening. Pack the seasoned vegetable mix tightly into the Mason jar, pressing down firmly with a spoon or masher to force out air pockets.

8. Slowly pour the brine liquid over the packed vegetables until completely submerged. Leave at least 1 inch of headspace at the top of the jar.

9. Place your jelly jar or glass fermentation weight on top of the vegetables to keep them weighed down beneath the brine.

10. Cover the jar mouth with your cheesecloth and secure it tightly with a rubber band or string so gases can escape during fermentation.

11. Set the jar on a plate or bowl to collect the overflow liquid. Allow the vegetables to ferment on your kitchen counter out of direct sunlight for 1-3 weeks. Check it daily and press down vegetables as needed to keep them submerged.

12. The fermentation is complete when the vegetables taste pickled and tangy. This could take 1-4 weeks, depending on variables. Regularly taste test after the first week. Refrigerate finished ferments - the probiotics remain active for months.

Be patient while the vegetables ferment. The length of fermentation depends on the vegetables, ambient temperature, and altitude. You will learn the ideal fermentation times for your conditions with practice.

Tips for Successful Fermentation

Here are helpful tips to guide your fermented creations to tastiness:

- Carefully measure brine ingredients for the proper 2 tbsp. salt per pound of vegetable ratio. This prevents pathogenic bacteria from growing while encouraging good bacteria.

- Keep vegetables submerged under the brine at all times. Use weights as needed and press them down daily.

- Ferment at average room temperatures between 60-75°F for best, consistent results. Avoid temperature extremes.

- Always allow gases to vent from the lid. Never seal fermentation jar lids completely airtight.

- Use glass, ceramic, or enamel vessels. Avoid reactive metals that can impart metallic flavors.

- Position jars away from direct sunlight, which can stall fermentation. Indirect light is beneficial.

- Allow vegetables to ferment for at least 1-3 weeks until nicely sour. Taste test after the first week.

- Trust your nose above all else. Discard foul or rancid-smelling ferments immediately for food safety.

Getting Creative with Lacto-Fermented Foods

Once you feel comfortable with the basics, have fun and get creative with ferments.

- Make mixed medleys with cabbage, carrots, beets, onions, cauliflower, etc.

- Try alternative vegetables like peppers, green beans, radishes, pumpkin, broccoli, etc.

- Mix in infinite combos of herbs, spices, garlic, ginger, chili, and more.

- Culture homemade salsa, pasta sauce, tamarind paste, lemons, and limes.

- Make beet, fruit scrap, or sourdough kvass by fermenting them in brine.

- Combine sauerkraut with apples and onions for a fermented chutney.

- Blend fermented vegetables into dips, salad dressings, soups, marinades, and smoothies.

- Use leftover brines for probiotic tonics, sodas, cocktail mixers, or vinaigrettes.

- Substitute lacto-ferments for vinegar in coleslaws, salad toppings, and condiments.

Easy and Delicious Pickling Recipes for Beginners

From crunchy dill spears and spicy pickled carrots to sweet relishes and easy refrigerator jalapenos, here's how to transform fresh garden ingredients into pickled delights.

Zippy Refrigerator Dill Pickles

These zippy dill spears come together for a quick pickle fix in just a few hours. One try, and you'll be hooked.

Ingredients:

- 1 lb. Kirby cucumbers
- 1 cup white vinegar
- 1 cup water
- 1 tbsp. salt
- 1 tbsp. sugar
- 1 tsp. dill seeds
- 4 garlic cloves, halved
- 1 tsp. black peppercorns

Instructions:

1. Wash cucumbers and slice into spears. Place in a quart jar.

2. Combine everything else in a small saucepan. Heat to boil, then remove from heat. Let it cool for 5 minutes.

3. Pour the brine over the cucumbers. Fridge for at least 3 hours, up to 2 weeks.

Bread and Butter Zucchini Pickles

These sweet and tangy quick pickles highlight summer's zucchini bounty.

Ingredients:

- 2 medium zucchinis, sliced 1/4" thick
- 1 medium onion, sliced thin
- 3/4 cup white vinegar
- 1/2 cup sugar
- 1 1/2 tsp. salt
- 1 tsp. mustard seeds
- 1/2 tsp. turmeric
- 1/4 tsp. celery seeds

Instructions:

1. Slice zucchini and onion. Place in a 1-quart jar.
2. Combine everything else in a small saucepan. Heat to boil.
3. Pour the hot brine over the vegetables. Cover and chill for at least 1 hour before eating. Store for up to 2 weeks.

Spicy Dilly Beans

These snappy pickled green beans packed with dill and garlic will surely be a hit.

Ingredients:

- 1 lb. fresh green beans, trimmed

- 3 garlic cloves, minced
- 1 cup white vinegar
- 1 cup water
- 1 1/2 tbsp. salt
- 1 tbsp. dried dill
- 1 tsp. red pepper flakes

Instructions:

1. Pack prepared beans and minced garlic into a 1-quart jar.

2. Combine everything else in a small saucepan. Heat just until boiling.

3. Pour the hot brine over the beans. Cover and chill for at least 2 hours before enjoying.

Classic Dill Pickles

These crunchy, old-fashioned canned dill pickles will be your new go-to for burgers and sandwiches. Once you taste homemade, you'll never go back.

Ingredients:

- 4 lb. Kirby cucumbers
- 6 cups white vinegar
- 6 cups water
- 1/4 cup pickling salt
- 12 garlic cloves, halved
- 1 tbsp. dill seeds

- 2 tsp. mustard seeds
- 4 dried red chili peppers (optional)

Instructions:

1. Wash quart jars and lids in hot, soapy water. Rinse well. Trim and cut cucumbers into spears.

2. In a saucepan, combine vinegar, water, and salt. Bring to a boil.

3. Add 3 garlic halves, 1/4 tsp. dill, and mustard seeds to each jar. Pack the cucumber spears tightly into the jars.

4. Ladle the hot brine over the cucumbers, leaving 1/2" headspace. Remove air bubbles. Wipe the rims clean.

5. Apply lids and ring finger tight bands. Process quart jars in a water bath canner for 10 minutes.

6. Cool the jars completely undisturbed. Check the seals, then store them for up to 1 year. Enjoy.

Bread and Butter Pickle Coins

Sweet, sour, and perfect on burgers, these canned pickle coins are irresistible.

Ingredients:

- 3 lb. cucumbers, sliced 1/4" thick
- 2 cups thin sliced onions
- 1/4 cup pickling salt
- 2 cups cider vinegar
- 2 cups sugar
- 2 tbsp. mustard seeds

- 1 tbsp. celery seeds
- 1 tsp. turmeric

Instructions:

1. Toss cucumber and onion slices with salt. Let it stand for 3 hours, then rinse and drain well.

2. In a saucepan, combine vinegar, sugar, and spices. Heat to boiling, stirring until the sugar dissolves.

3. Pack the veggies tightly into quart jars. Ladle in the hot brine, leaving 1/2" headspace. Wipe the rims. Apply the lids.

4. Process quart jars in a water bath canner for 10 minutes. Cool, completely undisturbed.

5. Check the seals, then store them for up to 1 year. Enjoy these classics on burgers, sandwiches, and more.

Sweet Gherkin Pickles

These petite, sweet pickles are so nostalgic. Enjoy them just like store-bought favorites.

Ingredients:

- 2 lb. pickling cucumbers
- 6 cups white vinegar
- 6 cups water
- 1/2 cup pickling salt
- 10 garlic cloves, halved
- 3 fresh dill sprigs
- 1 tbsp. mixed pickling spice

Instructions:

1. Wash pint jars and lids in hot, soapy water. Rinse well.

2. Wash the mini cucumbers. Vertically pack them into sterilized jars.

3. Combine vinegar, water, salt, and spice in a saucepan. Simmer for 5 minutes.

4. Add 3 garlic halves and 1 dill sprig to each jar.

5. Carefully ladle the hot brine over the cucumbers, leaving 1/2" headspace. Wipe the rims clean. Apply the lids.

6. Process the pint jars in a water bath canner for 10 minutes. Cool completely.

7. Check the seals, then store the sealed jars for up to 1 year. Enjoy.

Corn Relish

This sweet relish highlights summer corn and spices. Fantastic on hot dogs, brats, and sandwiches.

Ingredients:

- 4 ears of corn, kernels cut off

- 1 small onion, diced

- 1 green bell pepper, diced

- 3/4 cup apple cider vinegar

- 1/4 cup sugar

- 1 tsp. salt

- 1/2 tsp. celery seeds

- 1/4 tsp. mustard powder

Instructions:

1. Mix corn kernels, onion, and bell pepper in a bowl.

2. Combine vinegar, sugar, salt, celery seeds, and mustard powder in a saucepan. Heat to boil.

3. Pour the vinegar mixture over the corn mixture. Cover and chill for at least 2 hours. Keeps for 1 week.

Zesty Zucchini Relish

This zingy relish packs garden fresh zucchini into every tasty bite. Fantastic on hot dogs, burgers, and tacos.

Ingredients:

- 5 cups diced zucchini
- 1 large onion, diced
- 1 red bell pepper, diced
- 2 jalapenos, seeded and minced
- 1 cup white vinegar
- 3/4 cup apple cider vinegar
- 1 cup sugar
- 2 tbsp. pickling salt
- 1 tbsp. mustard seeds
- 1 tsp. celery seeds

Instructions:

1. Chop the veggies and place them in a large bowl.

2. Combine the vinegar, sugar, salt, mustard, and celery seeds in a saucepan over medium heat. Heat to boiling.

3. Pack the veggies tightly into pint jars. Ladle in the hot brine, leaving 1/2" headspace.

4. Release air bubbles with a chopstick. Wipe the rims clean. Apply the lids and rings.

5. Process the pint jars in a water bath canner for 15 minutes. Cool completely before storing. Enjoy.

Green Tomato Chutney

This tangy chutney highlights green tomatoes and spices. It's yummy, served with grilled meats or stirred into rice dishes.

Ingredients:

- 2 lb. green tomatoes, diced
- 1 onion, diced
- 1 green apple, diced
- 1 cup white vinegar
- 1/2 cup brown sugar
- 1 tbsp. grated ginger
- 2 tsp. salt
- 1 tsp. mustard seeds
- 1/2 tsp. allspice
- 1/4 tsp. cayenne pepper

Instructions:

1. In a large saucepan, combine all ingredients. Bring to a boil over medium heat.

2. Reduce the heat and simmer uncovered for 45 minutes until thickened.

3. Spoon into sterilized half-pint jars, leaving 1/2" headspace. Wipe the rims clean. Apply the lids.

4. Process the jars in a boiling water canner for 10 minutes.

5. Cool, completely undisturbed. Check seals, then store for up to 1 year. Enjoy.

Fruited Jalapeno Jelly

This sweet and spicy jelly makes a quick appetizer or gift from the garden.

Ingredients:

- 10 oz. jalapenos, seeded and chopped
- 1 red bell pepper, seeded and chopped
- 1-1/2 cups white vinegar
- 6 cups sugar
- 3 oz. liquid pectin
- 1/4 tsp. butter (optional)
- 1/2 tsp. crushed red pepper
- 1/2 cup dried cranberries

Instructions:

1. Puree the chopped peppers with vinegar in a blender until smooth. Pour into a saucepan.

2. Add sugar, pectin, optional butter, and crushed red pepper. Heat to a rolling boil over high heat, stirring constantly.

3. Once boiling, add the cranberries. Return to a boil and boil hard for 1 minute, stirring constantly.

4. Remove from heat. Carefully ladle into half-pint jars, leaving 1/4" headspace. Wipe the rims. Apply the lids.

5. Process the jars in a boiling water canner for 10 minutes. Cool completely. Check seals.

6. Store the sealed jars for up to 1 year. Refrigerate after opening. Enjoy with crackers, meats, cheese, and more.

Chapter 4: Pickling Techniques: Beyond Fermentation

Continue reading if you want to level up your pickling skills beyond just fermenting. This chapter explores the art of quick pickling with vinegar.

7. All types of vinegar can be used for quick pickling. Source: https://unsplash.com/photos/a-bottle-of-extra-virgin-olive-oil-sitting-on-a-cutting-board-ip4gwG2lpd4?utm_content=creditShareLink&utm_medium=referral&utm_source=unsplash

You'll learn how vinegar's acidic punch can transform veggies and fruits into tangy delights without a long fermentation process. You'll learn easy refrigerator pickling techniques for making jars of crunchy, full-flavored pickles using vinegar, salt, and aromatics you fancy.

You'll uncover how to craft custom brines by tinkering with different kinds of vinegar, spices, salts, and sweeteners to create your signature flavor combos. Whether you like sweet bread and butter pickles, dilly green beans, curried cauliflower, or kimchi-style, your brine options are infinite.

Introduction to Vinegar-Based Pickling

Vinegar pickling is a method of preserving and infusing foods like vegetables, fruits, eggs, and some meats in an acidic vinegar brine. It originated as a food preservation technique before refrigeration was widely available.

The acetic acid in vinegar inhibits dangerous bacteria and microorganisms' growth, allowing perishable foods to be safely preserved with a pickled, tangy flavor. Vinegar pickling adds dynamic flavor while extending the fresh produce's shelf life.

How Does Vinegar Pickling Work?

There are a few keys to how vinegar transforms fresh ingredients through pickling:

- Produce, or other foods are submerged into a brine of vinegar, water, salt, and aromatics like spices.

- Vinegar's acetic acid permeates the plant or animal tissues, lowering the pH and providing antimicrobial protection.

- Given time in the acidic brine, the food takes on bright, tangy, pickled characteristics.

- Once sufficiently pickled, foods can be refrigerated or processed in a water bath canner for shelf stability.

Vinegar pickling happens much more rapidly than traditional fermented pickling. The acetic acid quickly infuses tissues, and the brine preserves, so no lengthy culturing time is required.

Benefits and Applications of Vinegar Pickling

Many benefits make vinegar pickling a useful technique:

- **Flavor Enhancement** - Vinegar pickling noticeably enhances and alters flavors, providing a tangy, salty, pickled taste.

- **Preservation** - Vinegar effectively inhibits bacteria growth, extending perishable foods' shelf life.

- **Convenience** - Quicker than fermenting, vinegar pickling lets you easily enjoy pickled flavors with less hands-on time.

- **Customization** - Tailor pickled flavors using different vinegar, spices, sweeteners, and foods.

- **Small Batches** - Requires little equipment to pickle small amounts quickly.

- **Nutrition** - Can help preserve nutrients in seasonal foods for enjoyment later. Provides probiotics when live-cultured.

- **Variety** - You can pickle an array of vegetables, fruits, proteins, and eggs.

As you can see, vinegar pickling is extremely versatile. You can pickle cucumbers, green beans, beets, onions, eggs, watermelon rinds, fruits like peaches, and much more. Vinegar pickling captures seasonal flavors for year-round enjoyment.

The Science behind Vinegar Pickling

Vinegar pickling works under two primary mechanisms:

1. Acidification

By significantly lowering the food's pH, the acetic acid in vinegar provides an environment uninhabitable for dangerous bacteria like botulism to grow. Most vinegars have a pH around 2-3 when undiluted.

2. Osmosis

The acetic acid in the brine draws water out of food tissues via osmosis. This dehydration process concentrates natural sugars and acids within the food, further lowering pH for preservation.

In addition, vinegar denatures proteins on the surface of food, creating a protective barrier to deter microbial growth.

These mechanisms make vinegar an excellent choice for food preservation and imparting an acidic tang.

Pickling Equipment and Ingredients

Vinegar pickling doesn't require much specialized equipment. Below are the basics:

- **Jars** - Clear glass mason jars allow you to monitor food throughout pickling. Always use new lids.

- **Lids** - Metal lids for canning, cheesecloth for fermenting-style pickling.

- **Vinegar** - Provides the important acetic acid to preserve and pickle foods reliably.

- **Water** - Dilutes vinegar to the desired acidity for safety and flavor.

- **Salt** - Draws moisture from produce for crisp texture. It also provides seasoning.

- **Sugar** - Provides balance to the tart vinegar. Any sweetener can be used.

- **Produce** - Almost any fruit, veggie, and protein can be pickled. Cucumbers, carrots, and green beans are popular starters.

- **Seasonings** - Tailor flavors with your favorite fresh or dried herbs, spices, garlic, peppers, etc.

- **Funnel** - Useful for neatly guiding food and brine into the jar.

- **Tongs** - Help securely grip jars for transfers.

Vinegar Varieties for Pickling

One of the joys of vinegar pickling is experiencing how different vinegars influence the flavor. Consider these common varieties:

- **White Vinegar** - Most commonly used, its clear color allows food colors to shine through.

- **Apple Cider Vinegar** - Provides fruity undertones and pairs well with fall produce.

- **Wine Vinegar** - Unique flavors of red or white wine come through.

- **Rice Vinegar** - Made from rice wine, it provides mild acidity and subtle sweetness.

- **Balsamic Vinegar** - Deep, rich flavor, but use it sparingly due to lower acidity.

- **Fruit Infused** - Flavored with fruit like blueberries and pineapple.

- **Coconut Vinegar** - Imparts light coconut flavor.

- **Malt Vinegar** - Made from malted barley, and provides earthy, beer-like flavors.

The possibilities are endless. Taste-test different vinegars to discover new favorites and flavor combinations. The vinegar makes the pickle.

Tips for Delicious Vinegar Pickles

Here are some tips for making tasty, safely pickled foods:

- Only use vinegar with at least 5% acidity to prevent botulism and spoilage.

- Weigh down produce to keep submerged in brines, preventing mold growth.

- Unless you use the water bath process, store finished pickles refrigerated.

- Start with trusted recipes before improvising as you gain experience.

- Clean produce very well and sanitize equipment. Use clean hands.

- If a pickle smells or looks off, don't take risks - discard it. Trust your senses.

The Endless Potential of Vinegar Pickling

As you can see, quick pickling with vinegar offers remarkable flavor possibilities. While traditional long-brined fermented pickles have their place, the flexibility and simplicity of vinegar brine create numerous opportunities for infusing foods with tangy zip.

Vinegar pickling lets you easily capture the essence of fresh seasonal produce before it goes bad. You can customize flavors to suit your taste. Before long, your pantry will be stocked with your unique, quick, pickled creations using this versatile technique.

Quick Pickling Methods for Crunchy Results

Crunchy pickles are one of life's simple pleasures. By quickly pickling fresh fruits and vegetables, you can sink your teeth into satisfyingly crisp, tangy pickles in no time. Quick pickling gives you a snappy texture and zesty pickled flavor without the long wait of traditional fermenting methods.

With the proper techniques, you can easily pickle produce at the peak of freshness and enjoy it with a satisfying crunch for weeks. Read on to learn expert tips and tricks for quick pickling success with mouthwateringly crisp results every time.

Choosing Produce for Maximum Crunch

The first step in a quick pickling adventure is selecting the right fresh ingredients. Opt for extremely firm produce at the perfect stage of ripeness for quick pickling with the crispiest possible texture.

For fruits like peaches and nectarines, tree-ripened is ideal. Avoid bruised or overripe specimens. Gently press the fruit to ensure it's completely firm without any soft spots. Smaller peaches and apricots are usually crisper.

Freshness and firmness are essential with vegetables like cucumbers, carrots, green beans, and asparagus. Look for produce with smooth, taut skin free of blemishes. Press or flex the vegetable to test for crispness. Avoid limpness or wrinkling, signs they have lost moisture and vital crispness.

When quick pickling cucumbers, choose unwaxed varieties specially grown for pickling. Kirby, Persian, and gherkin cucumber cultivars have a naturally crunchy flesh perfect for the brine. Go for the smallest, youngest cucumbers, ideally 3 to 6 inches long. The smaller size means they've had less time on the vine to develop the cell wall-softening enzymes activated by pickling.

For carrots, select smaller, slender specimens. Larger, more mature carrots have a woodier core that remains tough even when quickly pickled. Carrot varieties like Nantes and Danvers have a deliciously crisp snap when young.

Look for thin asparagus spears, ideally no thicker than a pencil. Thinner stalks will quickly and evenly absorb the brine for a delicate, crunchy texture. Choose bright, perky-looking spears with tightly closed tips.

Pick pencil-sized green beans for tender snap. Pass on thick, more mature beans with tough skins and seedy centers. Seek beans bred for pickling, like the Salty cultivar.

When quick pickling onions, small spring onions or pearl onions work best, as their thinner skins allow even quicker brine penetration. Full-size onions also work if peeled first. Avoid soft or sprouting onions, which lack the ideal crunch.

No matter what you're quick pickling, uniform sizing helps ensure even brining and crisping. Pick fruits and vegetables as close in size as possible for best results.

Preparing Produce for Crisp, Snappy Texture

To retain that prized crunch when quick pickling, it's essential to prep your fresh produce properly before it ever hits the brine.

Gently wash vegetables under cool running water to remove dirt or debris without compromising their delicate flesh. Avoid soaking, which can cause texture-damaging waterlogging.

Use a clean, sharp knife and cutting board reserved only for vegetables to prevent cross-contamination. Slice produce into uniform 1/4 to 1/2 inch sticks, disks, or spears so the brine can penetrate quickly and evenly. Very large pieces may stay tough and unpickled in the center. Super thin cuts can over-soften. Keeping size uniform allows the produce to brine at the same rate.

Trim off blemished outer leaves or stems. For example, slice off tough asparagus ends, stem ends of cucumbers, or roots and stem tips of onions or carrots. This prevents unwanted tough sections in your finished pickles.

Consider peeling waxy skins that may not soften sufficiently during quick pickling. Shedding the skin helps the brine work magic for an evenly crisp texture. Produce like beets, turnips, pearl onions, and even firm pears benefit from peeling before pickling.

Work swiftly and minimize exposure to air when prepping produce to prevent enzymatic softening. Have your chilled brine ready to go in the fridge. Pack the produce into jars and cover it entirely with cold brine as soon as it is sliced to your desired size: the less handling time, the more crisper your pickles.

Chilling for Improved Crispness

Temperature control is one of the secrets to optimally crunchy pickled results. Keeping everything as cold as possible short-circuits the natural softening enzymes in fruits and vegetables so that your quick pickles stay satisfyingly snappy.

Chill all your quick pickling ingredients before getting started. Refrigerate washed produce until completely cold. Also, store jars, lids, spices, vinegar, and other supplies in the refrigerator. Use ice water to rinse and further crisp cut vegetables before packing the jars.

Make your brine nice and cold. Combine room temperature vinegar and spices, then heat only to dissolve the salt and awaken flavors. Remove from heat and allow the brine to thoroughly chill in the refrigerator before pouring it over the prepared raw vegetables and fruits. Never use hot brine, as heat dramatically accelerates softening enzymes.

Work in the coolest part of your kitchen to prevent even minimal exposure to warmth during the quick pickling process. Chill the jars in the fridge while preparing the other ingredients.

Once your produce is packed into jars and covered with the chilled brine, immediately move the filled jars back to the refrigerator. Quickly getting your sealed jars into the cold prevents the loss of that valuable crunch.

Maximizing Crunch with the Perfect Brine

The brine solution is the critical player in a pickling operation. When formulated properly, the brine transforms crisp produce into snappy, pickled form as it penetrates the plant cells. Follow these tips for the ideal brine for crunchy, quick pickle success:

- Use vinegar for tang and preserving power. Avoid harsh distilled white and opt for mild rice wine or apple cider vinegar. Add it gradually until the brine is pleasantly tart but not abrasive. Too little acidity risks poor preservation and mushy texture.

- Add salt progressively until the ideal balance of flavor enhancement and firmness develops. Kosher and pickling salt work well. Stop when the brine tastes pleasantly salty yet light. Excess salt can toughen texture.

- Limit added sugar, which counteracts vinegar's preservative properties for crispness. A teaspoon or two of sugar removes harshness, but don't overdo it.

- Bloom spices, garlic, peppercorns, bay leaves, and other flavor elements by heating briefly in the brine until fragrant before chilling.

- Cool the brine completely before using. Hot brine causes vegetables and fruits to give up their natural pectins, enzymes, and juices, resulting in a mushier final pickle.

- Gently skim off the scum of vegetable matter or seeds that float to the top of the brine after initial contact. Skimming removes cell wall-softening enzymes.

- Fine strain the brine through cheesecloth to remove solid bits. Particles can leave an unwanted mushy texture. Straining yields crystal clear brine for attractive presentation.

Handling Produce Gently for Optimal Crispness

Once submerged in brine, quick pickles are sensitive souls for retaining that characteristic crunch. Gentleness is key from the packing stage through storage.

Arranging trimmed vegetable spears vertically in jars allows you to slip them neatly into the brine solution with minimal handling. Fold them gently into the brine rather than shaking or pressing down. Excessive jostling causes vegetable cell rupture, initiating the softening process.

When pouring chilled brine into filled jars, aim to have it run gently down the insides rather than directly hitting the produce. This prevents bruising fragile flesh. Slide a plastic chopstick or knife down the inside of packed jars after pouring in brine to dislodge trapped air pockets. Bubbles of air lead to limp pickles, so make sure the brine penetrates completely.

Once sealed, avoid agitating or shaking filled jars. As enzymes work slowly to dissolve pectins and cellulose, vibration accelerates softening. Transport jars carefully, cushioning with dishtowels in the refrigerator or coolers. Steady conditions lead to steady crispness.

Before serving or gifting your quick pickles, press on the sides of the jar to detect worrying soft spots. Briefly unsealing and sampling a pickle helps avoid disappointing anyone with a mushy forkful. Enjoy pickles within a few weeks before the brine destroys the texture.

Storing Quick Pickles for Extended Crunch

Preserving that satisfying crunch means storing your quick pickles properly after jarring. Follow these guidelines:

- Keep refrigerated pickles chilled at all times. Fridge temperatures slow down the natural enzymes that cause softening over the long haul. Quick pickles sealed in jars will maintain peak crispness for 1-3 months refrigerated.

- For crisp texture up to a year after quick pickling, can the sealed jars in a water bath according to canning guidelines. This heat processing kills bacteria for extended shelf life unrefrigerated.

- Freezing is another long-term storage method, halting enzymatic action for at least 1 year. Thaw jars slowly in the fridge before eating to rejuvenate crispiness closer to just-pickled results.

- Minimize light exposure during storage to prevent pickle color and vitamin content loss. Store in cool, dark places like the back of the fridge or pantry.

- Avoid temperature fluctuations. Don't store jars above 95°F or let them freeze and thaw repeatedly. Heat and cold hasten the decline of crispness.

- Enjoy your crunchy, quick pickle creations within a few weeks for the very best texture and tangy, bright flavor. You can keep that satisfying snap for many months when they are stored properly.

Expanding beyond Cucumbers for More Quick Pickled Crunch

Don't limit your quick pickling adventures to cucumbers alone. Almost any firm, fresh vegetable or fruit can be transformed into a tangy pickle with a deliciously crisp bite.

- Hard, round carrots become sweet, earthy, quick pickles when cut into coins, sticks, or matchsticks. Their hardy texture holds up beautifully to a quick brining. Chill them in ice water for extra crunch before packing them into jars.

- Trim green beans and quickly pickle them whole for a pretty presentation. Choose slender, petite beans for a delicate crunch that's perfect with fish or roasted meats. Just the tips of large beans can be pickled for a crisp contrast on the plate.

- Asparagus, green onions, and okra have an affinity for quick pickling, retaining their satisfying snap when briefly brined. Peel and slice firm or Asian pears into thin wedges for a sweet-tart pickle perfect on cheese boards.

- Quick pickled beets are delightful treats, as vinegar minimizes their tendency to bleed and lose texture. Peaches and nectarines hold their shape beautifully when quickly pickled to capture the height of summer in a jar.

For a delicious crunch in all seasons, keep your crisper drawer stocked with fresh produce perfect for quick pickling. With the techniques you've learned, you can easily preserve the satisfying snap of any vegetable or fruit and enjoy it for weeks. The possibilities for creating your signature quick pickled condiments are endless.

Creating Diverse Pickling Brines for Various Flavors

The brine solution is the key to infusing fruits, vegetables, and proteins with delicious, pickled flavor. You can create an array of distinctive pickle profiles beyond basic dills by exploring different brine ingredients. Follow the guidelines below to craft diverse brines to add unique flavors to your quick pickles.

Tailoring Brine Strength

Carefully balancing brine ingredients gives you control over the flavor profile.

Adjusting Acidity

The brine's acidity comes from vinegar, which simultaneously infuses flavor and preserves the pickles. White distilled vinegar provides clean tartness that won't overpower other seasonings. For a more complex flavor, use apple cider or rice vinegar. Start with a smaller amount of vinegar and taste as you increase it gradually. Stop when the brine is pleasantly sour but not aggressively tart.

Controlling Saltiness

Salt enhances other flavors and firms up the pickled produce's texture. Table salt is acceptable, but canning or kosher salt will integrate more smoothly. Start with moderate salt according to recipes, then tweak to suit your preferences. Remember, you can always add more later if the brine tastes under-salted.

Balancing with Natural Sweeteners

Add a touch of sugar, honey, maple syrup, or other natural sweetener to mellow tartness. Start with only a teaspoon or two per cup of brine. You want a hint of sweetness to round out flavors, not overpower them. Taste and incrementally add as needed.

Diluting Intensity

For milder brines, replace a bit of the vinegar with water, vegetable broth, or tea. Start by swapping out 2 tablespoons of vinegar per cup of brine and add more liquid until you achieve the desired acidity level.

Infusing Herbs, Spices, and Aromatics

Fresh and dried seasonings let you create ethnic flavor profiles or new fusions.

Building Around Fresh Herbs

Basil, dill, cilantro, and mint give the brines a vibrant, garden-fresh character. Use about 1/4 cup loosely packed whole sprigs per 2 cups of brine. Bruise or crush herbs to release their essential oils.

Punching up Flavor with Dried Spices

Warming spices like coriander, mustard seeds, and red pepper bring excitement to a brine. Add 1 teaspoon of smaller seeds or 1/2 teaspoon of larger seeds per cup of brine. Crush or grind them for a more intense flavor release.

Harnessing Aromatics

Sliced onions, garlic, ginger, and chili peppers provide a flavor foundation. Cook them briefly in vinegar before adding other ingredients to mellow their raw edge. Start with 2 to 3 tablespoons per batch of brine.

Trying International Combos

Create global flavors like Indian pickles with mustard seed, fenugreek, and turmeric or Mexican-style escabeche with jalapeños, cumin, and oregano.

Developing Original Spice Blends

Craft unique flavor medleys like lemon rosemary or orange-vanilla-cardamom brines. Dare to get creative with spices and let your palate guide you.

Boosting Flavor with Extras

Supplementary ingredients layered into the brine provide flavor depth.

Intensifying with Alliums

Sautéed onions and roasted garlic lend savory undertones to brines. Add 1/4 cup onion and 2 cloves garlic per 2 cups of brine.

Building Umami with Soy Sauce

A splash of soy sauce intensifies the overall flavor. Start with 1 teaspoon per cup of brine and adjust to suit your taste buds.

Adding Subtle Richness with Oil

Swirling in a small amount of olive or vegetable oil provides a hint of roundness. Drizzle in 1 to 2 teaspoons of oil per batch and emulsify.

Contributing Brightness with Citrus

Juice or zest from lemons, limes, grapefruit, or oranges punctuate brines with fresh citrusy notes. Start with 1 to 2 tablespoons of juice per cup of brine.

Invigorating with Chilies

Minced hot peppers, chili paste, or hot sauce inject thrilling heat. Habañeros, Thai chilies, and jalapeños are great choices. Add them by the 1/4 teaspoon to start.

Building Body with Tomato

Chopped or pureed tomatoes lend subtle savory flavor and color. Start with 2 to 3 tablespoons of crushed tomatoes per cup of brine.

Adding Earthiness with Beer

Non-hoppy beer, like a lager, provides nuanced maltiness. Substitute 1/4 cup beer for an equal amount of vinegar.

Adjusting Flavors

- Taste as you go to achieve your perfect brine balance.

- Add more vinegar, a teaspoon at a time, if the brine lacks puckery tartness.

- Increase salt gradually if the overall flavor is flat or dull.

- Stir in a bit of sugar if bitterness or harsh acidity needs softening.

- Brew a tea bag of ginger, peppercorns, or other spices directly in the brine to intensify their flavor.

- Skim off scum after an hour of contact with the vegetables to remove impurities that can cause off-flavors.

Don't be afraid to experiment, and trust your tastebuds. Seasoned picklers develop signature brines reflecting their unique flavor sensibilities. With the endless possible ingredient combinations, you can create diverse brines tailored to suit any pickle palette.

Pickling Different Vegetables and Fruits

Certain brine formulations pair well with various produce.

Pickling Cucumbers

Use vinegar, salt, and fresh dill brine for classic dill pickles. Optionally add garlic, peppercorns, coriander, or mustard seeds. Use sweetener, turmeric, and mustard seeds for bread and butter chips.

Green Beans

Accentuate their fresh flavor with simple brines focused on vinegar, salt, and aromatics like onion, garlic, and bell pepper.

Carrots

8. Carrots can be pickled with warm spices. Source: https://unsplash.com/photos/baby-carrots-fcgPRZmTM5w?utm_content=creditShareLink&utm_medium=refe rral&utm_source=unsplash

Warm spices like cinnamon, clove, allspice, and ginger complement their natural sweetness. Citrus notes from orange or lemon zest brighten up the brine.

Asparagus

The delicate flavor is brought out with light brines made from rice vinegar, lemon, and savory seasonings like tarragon or fennel.

Beets

Orange, ginger, and coriander seeds magnify their earthy sweetness. A splash of vodka helps beets retain their vibrant color.

Peaches

For sweet-tart pickled peaches, use a sugar-sweetened brine with a peach or berry-flavored vinegar and aromatics like cinnamon sticks and vanilla.

Eggs

Brine hard-boiled eggs in a bold mixture of soy sauce, tea, and warm spices like star anise and smoked paprika for intensely flavored pickled eggs.

Green Tomatoes

Accentuate their crisp sourness with cider vinegar, garlic, pickling spice, and a touch of maple syrup or honey for balance.

Mix and match produce with creative brines until you find combinations that make your tastebuds tingle. Keep experimenting with new brining ingredients and allow your inspiration to guide you.

Testing Finished Pickles

Once the pickles have had time to soak and mingle in the brine, always follow these steps:

1. Inspect pickles for desired doneness. Leave spears or chunks in the brine longer if still too firm.

2. Fish out a pickle and sample it. Ensure the flavors taste balanced, not too harsh, salty, or strong.

3. Try the pickle for the intended use, like on a sandwich or salad. See how the flavors blend with other ingredients.

4. Observe how the brined produce holds up texture-wise. It should retain an appealing crunch without mushiness unless deliberately softened.

5. Tweak brines as needed. Add more vinegar for tang or sweetener to tone down tartness. Water down strong brines.

6. Let pickles sit overnight to meld flavors after adjusting brines. The brine and produce should marry into ideal taste harmony.

Preparing Exotic Global Pickling Brines

In addition to basic dill, explore the many international pickle preparations.

Korean Kimchi

This spicy fermented pickle starts with a salty brine punched with Korean red pepper, minced garlic, ginger, fish sauce, rice flour, and sliced vegetables like cabbage or radish.

Indian Lime Pickle

Whole limes and chilies pickle in a pungent oil-based brine of fenugreek, turmeric, cumin, and other warming spices. Mustard seeds add texture.

German Sauerkraut

Salt-brined cabbage ferments into the quintessential sour pickle optionally spiked with caraway seeds. Rinse cabbage first to limit overly sour flavor.

Japanese Tsukemono

Napa cabbage, radishes, cucumber, and other vegetables are salted, rinsed, and pressed to draw out their moisture before pickling in a light rice vinegar brine.

Polish Dill Ogórki

Cucumbers in vinegar brine absorb the flavor of abundant dill, garlic, and spices for a classic Eastern European pickle.

Italian Giardiniera

A pickled mixed vegetable medley featuring cauliflower, carrots, celery, and peppers in a brine of vinegar and chili pepper.

Mexican Escabeche

Thinly sliced carrots, onions, and jalapeños quick-pickled in a vinegary brine highlighted with citrus, cumin, and oregano.

Immerse your senses in new flavors by preparing your versions of traditional global pickling brines. With some thoughtful experimentation, you can create completely novel fusions.

Chapter 5: Fermented Vegetable Recipes for Beginners

In this chapter, you'll discover the tangy crunch of homemade fermented vegetables. Step-by-step instructions walk you through basic sauerkraut and kimchi recipes made probiotic-rich through lactic acid fermentation. You'll learn simple pickling techniques for fermenting diverse vegetables like radishes, beets, and green beans. Spice blends and brines let you build global flavor profiles from Korean kimchi to German sauerkraut. Once comfortable with the process, incorporate nutritious fermented veggies into everyday dishes, from breakfast tacos to salad toppings.

9. Kimchi is a fermented vegetable. Source: AhmadElq, CC BY-SA 4.0 <https://creativecommons.org/licenses/by-sa/4.0>, via Wikimedia Commons: https://commons.wikimedia.org/wiki/File:Korean_Kimchi.jpg

Simple Sauerkraut and Kimchi Recipes

Sauerkraut and kimchi are flavorful fermented vegetables packed with probiotics. Making them at home is easy and fun, with only a few basic ingredients and steps. Here are beginner-friendly recipes for tasty sauerkrauts and kimchis you can feel good about eating.

Classic Sauerkraut

This basic sauerkraut recipe transforms cabbage into a tangy, crispy fermented probiotic powerhouse. Enjoy it as a condiment or side dish.

Ingredients:

- 1 medium-head green cabbage
- 1 1/2 tbsp. kosher salt
- 1 tbsp. caraway seeds (optional)
- 4 oz. glass jar with lid

Instructions:

1. Shred the cabbage thinly and place it in a large bowl. Sprinkle salt over the top and massage it into the cabbage until liquid is released.

2. Pack the cabbage tightly into the jar, pressing down firmly to remove air pockets. Add caraway seeds if desired. Pour the liquid released from the cabbage into the jar.

3. Seal the jar loosely and allow it to ferment at room temperature for 3-10 days until it reaches the desired sourness. Check daily and press down the cabbage to keep it submerged.

4. Once fermented to taste, tighten the lid and refrigerate to slow the fermentation. Enjoy for up to 6 months.

Juniper Sauerkraut

Juniper berries lend a woodsy flavor to this unique twist on classic sauerkraut.

Ingredients:

- 1 medium-head green cabbage
- 1 1/2 tbsp. kosher salt
- 2 tsp. juniper berries
- 4 oz. glass jar with lid

Instructions:

1. Thinly shred the cabbage and transfer it to a large bowl. Sprinkle salt over the cabbage and massage until liquid releases.

2. Add the juniper berries. Using your hands, tightly pack the cabbage mixture into the jar, pressing down to remove air pockets. Top with the liquid released.

3. Seal the jar loosely and let it ferment at room temperature for 3-10 days until sufficiently sour. Check daily and press the cabbage down to keep it submerged.

4. When fermented to taste, tighten the lid and refrigerate to slow the fermentation. Enjoy juniper-infused sauerkraut up to 6 months.

Simple Kimchi

This easy beginner kimchi recipe delivers a light spicy-sour flavor with only a few ingredients.

Ingredients:

- 1 lb. napa cabbage, chopped
- 1 tbsp. kosher salt
- 1 green onion, chopped

- 1 tbsp. ginger, minced
- 1 tsp. red pepper flakes

Instructions:

1. Sprinkle salt over the cabbage in a large bowl. With clean hands, massage and squeeze the cabbage until it softens and releases liquid, about 5 minutes.

2. Add the green onion, ginger, and red pepper flakes. Mix thoroughly to distribute ingredients evenly.

3. Firmly pack the cabbage mixture into a quart-sized jar. Pour the liquid released from the cabbage over the top. Seal the jar loosely.

4. Ferment at room temperature for 3-5 days until the kimchi reaches your desired tangy-spicy flavor. Check daily and press down the cabbage to keep it fully submerged.

5. When fermented to taste, tightly seal the jar and refrigerate to pause fermentation. Consume within 2 months.

Radish Kimchi

This easy kimchi highlights the spicy bite of radishes for a quick ferment.

Ingredients:

- 1 lb. radishes, thinly sliced
- 1 tbsp. kosher salt
- 1 green onion, chopped
- 1 tsp. fresh grated ginger

- 1 tbsp. rice vinegar

- 1 tsp. of gochugaru or red pepper flakes

Instructions:

1. Place the radish slices in a bowl and sprinkle with salt. Massage for 2-3 minutes until slightly softened and juicy.

2. Add the green onion, ginger, vinegar, and gochugaru. Mix thoroughly to combine.

3. Firmly pack the radish mixture into a pint-sized jar. Pour the released liquid over the top. Loosely seal.

4. Let it ferment at room temperature for 2-3 days until it reaches the desired piquant flavor. Keep the radish pieces submerged in liquid.

5. Tighten the lid and move the jar to the refrigerator for long-term storage. Enjoy spicy pickled radishes for up to 4 months.

Spicy Kimchi Stew

This hearty stew turns kimchi into a delicious one-pot meal.

Ingredients:

- 2 tbsp. vegetable oil

- 1 onion, diced

- 2 cloves garlic, minced

- 2 cups kimchi, chopped

- 4 cups vegetable broth

- 2 medium potatoes, cubed

- 1 block of firm tofu, cubed

- Sesame oil for serving

- Steamed rice for serving

Instructions:

Heat vegetable oil in a large pot over medium heat. Cook the onion for 5 minutes until translucent. Add garlic and cook 1 minute more.

1. Add the kimchi, broth, potatoes, and tofu. Bring to a boil, then reduce heat and simmer for 20 minutes until the potatoes are tender.

2. Serve the stew over steamed rice, drizzled with a little sesame oil.

Spicy Kimchi Cheese Toast

Kimchi's flavor perfectly balances melted cheese in this quick breakfast.

Ingredients:

- 2 slices whole grain bread

- 2 tbsp. butter, softened

- 2 oz. cheddar cheese, shredded

- 1/4 cup kimchi, chopped

- 1 green onion, sliced

Instructions:

1. Spread 1 tablespoon butter on each slice of bread. Place the slices buttered-side down in a skillet over medium heat.

2. Divide the cheese evenly between the 2 slices. Cook for 2-3 minutes until bottom is golden brown.

3. Flip both slices over. Top the cheese side of each toast with half of the kimchi and green onions.

4. Continue cooking for 1-2 minutes until the cheese melts. Remove from heat and enjoy.

Sauerkraut Bacon Deviled Eggs

Sauerkraut gives these party favorites a probiotic boost.

Ingredients:

- 6 hard-boiled eggs, peeled and halved lengthwise
- 1/4 cup mayonnaise
- 1 tbsp. Dijon mustard
- 2 tbsp. sauerkraut, finely chopped
- 2 slices cooked bacon, crumbled
- Smoked paprika for garnish

Instructions:

1. Scoop the egg yolks from the halved whites into a bowl. Set the egg white halves on a serving platter.

2. Mash the yolks with mayonnaise and mustard until smooth and creamy. Mix in sauerkraut and bacon crumbles.

3. Spoon or pipe the filling back into the egg whites. Dust with smoked paprika.

4. Chill for 1 hour to allow flavors to meld before serving.

Fermented Pickles with Diverse Flavor Profiles

Fermenting vegetables into live-cultured pickles preserves them and develops complex flavors beyond basic sourness. This section provides recipes for crafting pickles with diverse global seasoning influences and unique ingredient combinations.

Once you master basic pickling techniques, use these recipes as inspiration for creating your signature flavor profiles.

Indian-Spiced Turmeric Cauliflower

Warm Indian spices accentuate cauliflower's nutty flavor in this golden pickle.

Ingredients:

- 1 head cauliflower, cut into small florets
- 1 tbsp. kosher salt
- 1 cup water
- 1 tsp. turmeric
- 1 tsp. mustard seeds
- 1 tsp. cumin seeds
- 1 tsp. coriander seeds
- 1 tsp. ginger, minced
- 1 serrano chili, sliced (optional)

Instructions:

1. Mix the cauliflower florets with salt in a large bowl and let sit for 30 minutes to draw out the liquid. Rinse the florets under cold water and drain well.

2. In a spice grinder, coarsely grind the turmeric, mustard, cumin, and coriander seeds.

3. Place the cauliflower into a 1-quart jar. Top with ground spices, ginger, and chili if using. Pour water over to cover.

4. Seal the jar loosely and ferment at room temperature for 3-5 days until sour to taste. Keep the cauliflower fully submerged.

5. For long-term storage, tighten the lid and refrigerate. Allow flavors to meld 1 week before eating.

Dilly Green Bean Pickles

Dill and garlic add a classic flavor to quickly fermented green beans.

Ingredients:

- 1 lb. green beans, trimmed
- 1 tbsp. kosher salt
- 2 cloves garlic, peeled and halved
- 1 tsp. dill seed
- 1 cup water

Instructions:

1. Massage salt into the green beans in a bowl for 2-3 minutes until they soften. Rinse the beans under cold water and drain well.

2. Tightly pack the green beans upright into a 1-quart jar. Top with garlic and dill seed. Pour water over the beans to cover completely.

3. Seal the jar loosely and ferment at room temperature for 2-3 days until soured to taste. Keep the beans submerged in brine throughout fermentation.

4. When pickled to your liking, tighten the lid and store the jar in the refrigerator. Allow flavors to meld 1 week before serving.

Kimchi-Style Fermented Radishes

This quick kimchi adds radish's peppery crunch to the classic Korean flavors.

Ingredients:

- 1 lb. radishes sliced thin
- 1 tbsp. kosher salt
- 2 scallions, chopped
- 1 tbsp. ginger, minced
- 1 tbsp. red pepper flakes
- 1/2 cup water

Instructions:

1. Place the radish slices in a bowl. Salt and massage them gently for 3 minutes until they soften and exude liquid.

2. Transfer to a 1-quart jar. Top with scallions, ginger, and red pepper flakes. Pour water over to cover.

3. Loosely seal the jar and allow it to ferment at room temperature for 1-3 days until it reaches the desired sour-spicy flavor.

4. For long-term storage, tighten the lid and refrigerate. Allow the flavors to meld for a few days before eating.

Maple-Bourbon Fermented Beets

Sweet maple and bourbon complement earthy beets in this unique fermented pickle.

Ingredients:

- 2 lb. beets peeled and cut into 1/2-inch wedges
- 1 tbsp. kosher salt
- 1 cup water
- 1/4 cup maple syrup
- 2 tbsp. bourbon

Instructions:

1. Layer the beet wedges in a 1-quart jar, sprinkling each layer evenly with salt. Pour water over the beets until completely covered.

2. Seal the jar loosely and ferment at room temperature for 4-7 days until the beets are sour to taste. Keep the beets submerged in brine.

3. Drain off the brine and transfer the beets to a clean jar. Add maple syrup and bourbon. Reseal and store in the refrigerator.

4. Allow flavors to meld 1 week before eating for the best flavor. Refrigerated, they will keep up to 4 months.

Fermented Giardiniera

This tangy Italian veggie mix makes an easy starter ferment.

Ingredients:

- 1 cup cauliflower florets
- 1 carrot, sliced 1/4-inch thick
- 1 celery stalk, sliced 1/4-inch thick
- 1/2 bell pepper, diced
- 2 cloves garlic, smashed
- 1 tbsp. kosher salt
- 1 cup water

Instructions:

1. Place prepped vegetables into a 1-quart jar. Top with smashed garlic cloves.

2. Dissolve salt in water and pour over vegetables until submerged. Seal the jar loosely.

3. Ferment at room temperature for 3-5 days until it reaches the desired sourness, keeping the vegetables weighed down.

4. Secure the lid and move the jar to the refrigerator for storage. Allow flavors to meld 1 week before eating.

Sauerkraut Kimchi Fusion

This creative ferment fuses German and Korean flavors into one powerhouse pickled vegetable.

Ingredients:

- 1 small head napa cabbage, chopped
- 1 tbsp. kosher salt
- 1 tbsp. ginger, minced
- 2 cloves garlic, minced
- 1 tbsp. caraway seeds
- 1 tsp. red pepper flakes

Instructions:

1. Place the cabbage in a large bowl. Massage salt into cabbage until slightly softened and juicy, about 5 minutes.

2. Add ginger, garlic, caraway seeds, and pepper flakes. Mix thoroughly to combine.

3. Firmly pack spiced cabbage into a 1-quart jar. Top with the liquid released from salting. Seal the jar.

4. Ferment at room temperature for 4-7 days until it reaches the desired tangy-spicy flavor. Press the cabbage down daily if needed.

5. For storage, tighten the lid and refrigerate. Allow the flavors to meld 1 week before eating.

Incorporating Fermented Vegetables into Everyday Meals

Luckily, it's easy and fun to incorporate more fermented veggies into your everyday meals. Here are a few excellent tips:

Ways to Enjoy Fermented Vegetables for Breakfast

Starting your day with fermented foods is a great habit for gut health. The natural probiotics help "reset" your digestive system. Here are some ideas for enjoying fermented vegetables at breakfast:

- In the morning, you may crave something savory. Kimchi, sauerkraut, or other fermented veggies can replace toast or cereal. Their tangy crunch wakes up your palate. For instance, try kimchi fried rice. Simply stir leftover rice with kimchi, sesame oil, and soy sauce. The umami flavors make a satisfying hot breakfast.

- If you prefer a cold start, create a yogurt parfait with layers of yogurt, granola, and shredded fermented vegetables, like beet kvass or carrot kraut. The earthy sweetness complements the creamy yogurt.

- Wake up your usual egg dishes by adding fermented touches. Stir kimchi, pickled onions, or curtido into scrambled eggs or omelets. Top your avocado toast with sauerkraut and a fried egg. Or craft a breakfast taco with kimchi, egg, cheese, and salsa wrapped in a warm tortilla.

- Looking for something lighter? Whip up a green smoothie with yogurt, fruit, greens, and a spoonful of fermented veggies, like ginger kvass or lemony preserved daikon. The tang balances the smoothie's natural sweetness.

- If you enjoy smoked salmon and bagels, mix things up by swapping the traditional cream cheese for a schmear of beet kvass or pickled onions. It adds a new dimension to the classic flavor pairing.

With a little creativity, adding a boost of fermented goodness into your morning meal routine is easy. The live cultures energize you from the inside out.

Simple Salads Enlivened with Fermentation

Crunchy, wholesome salads are a perfect way to consume your daily dose of fermented fare. Their bright flavors and textures liven up greens and veggies.

10. Salads are a good way to consume your daily dose of fermented food. Source: https://www.pexels.com/photo/vegetable-salad-on-plate-1059905/

- Toss beet, carrot, or ginger kvass into a simple green salad. Their tang plays nicely against bitter greens while adding color. Top the salad with yogurt or kefir dressing blended with herbs for a creamy element.

- Take coleslaw up a notch by using thinly sliced fermented cabbage and shredded carrots instead of the plain varieties. The contents of the jar make an instant probiotic-packed slaw. Add mustard, mayo, or vinaigrette and toss to coat.

- Vietnamese salads like papaya or green mango pair well with fermented shrimp or fish paste. This umami garnish adds flavor. Or use fermented bean curd or soybeans instead of regular tofu.

- Thinly shaved vegetables, like fennel, carrots, and celery, become next level when quick-pickled or soaked in brine overnight. Toss them in bright, acidic dressings for a tangy crunch.

- Don't forget protein. Salmon, chicken, tofu, and lentils blend seamlessly into salad bowls boosted with fermented touches. Sprinkle kimchi croutons over the top for even more probiotic goodness.

The possibilities are endless when constructing salads with fermented add-ins. They balance flavor and texture while maximizing nutritional content.

Fermented Twists on Sandwiches and Wraps

Do you want to spice up your usual sandwich or wrap routine? Fermented vegetables add flavorful punches to lunchtime favorites.

- Pair cured meats like salami or prosciutto with quick-pickled vegetables like onions, carrots, radishes, or fennel. Layer the ingredients between crusty bread or roll them into a wrap. The fermented crunch balances the rich meats.

- Vinegar-based slaws made with fermented cabbage or cucumbers lend brightness to heavy sandwiches. Think pastrami on rye piled with sauerkraut instead of Swiss, or shaved turkey with crisp curtido slaw and avocado.

- Stir miso into mayonnaise to create an umami spread, then use it in place of plain mayo or mustard. Try it on roasted vegetable sandwiches or classic deli combos like ham and cheese. The nutty sweetness enhances standard sandwiches.

- Kimchi's depth pairs wonderfully with melted cheese. Create a fusion grilled cheese by adding kimchi and a spread of miso mayo between bread.

- For a portable meal, wrap up your favorite taco fillings in a tortilla with typical fixings, plus pickled carrots, radishes, onions, or jalapeños. The fermented veggie crunch makes tacos and burritos even more craveable.

With creativity and an open mind, sandwiches become vehicles for tasty, fermented additions like miso mayo, quick pickles, and kimchi that make lunchtime vibrant.

Noodles and Grains Elevated by Fermentation

Fermented foods transform boring bowls of noodles, grains, and legumes into crave-worthy meals. Their tangy crunch adds a dimension of texture and flavor.

- Drain and rinse canned chickpeas, then toss them with minced garlic, olive oil, and sauerkraut. The briny sweetness makes a delicious plant-based topping for pasta or grain bowls.

- Add a spoonful of miso paste and chopped kimchi to instant noodles while cooking for a quick ramen hack.

Mix in spinach, mushrooms, or eggs, too. The deep umami flavor punches up the entire bowl.

- Bibimbap and poke bowls pop with fermented daikon, soy sauce, kimchi, and a seasoned over-easy egg on top. The interplay of hot and cold textures with briny tang is highly addictive.

- Plain rice and lentils become intriguing meals when cooked with sauerkraut, topped with a dollop of beet kvass, or served with spicy curtido. The ferments provide contrasts of flavor and temperature.

- Even basic pasta gets an upgrade when tossed with oil, herbs, Parmesan, and salty preserved lemons or mixed olives. Their sharp brightness cuts through the rich, starchy noodles.

Grains, noodles, and legumes are the perfect blank canvas for pickled, preserved, and fermented ingredients. Add them liberally to boost nutrition and taste in one delightful swoop.

Savory Soups and Stews with Fermented Flair

Warm up with soups and stews punctuated by pungent fermented ingredients as the temperature drops. They add a comforting flavor to steaming bowls.

- Stir a spoonful of miso paste into a broth-based soup at the end to contribute warm umami without overcooking the tender probiotics. Try it in ramen, pho, egg drop, or vegetable noodle soups.

- Sauerkraut complements hearty bean and lentil stews. Add it in the last 5 minutes of cooking to retain the beneficial live cultures. If using heavily salted sauerkraut, rinse it first to reduce sodium.

- Add a garnish of fermented vegetables like pickled carrots, radishes, or jalapeños to creamy potato soups. Their crunch and zing cut through the richness. Alternatively, finish the soup with a drizzle of mustard made with fermented ingredients.

- Chili and chowders sing with a garnish of kimchi, curtido, or curtido. Their vinegary spice and acidity balance the thicker textures and heavier flavors. Stir them in at the end to retain their microbial potency.

- Miso's deep savoriness can intensify flavors when stirred into soups, particularly vegetarian broths and tomato-based varieties. A little goes a long way, so add it in increments until you achieve the perfect umami flavor.

When the weather turns cold, embrace the therapeutic power of steaming soups and stews punched with probiotic-packed fermented foods. They truly are comfort in a bowl.

Liven up Dinner with Tangy Ferments

Dinnertime is a chance to get adventurous with fermented vegetables as ingredients. They make every meal prep even more nourishing and tasty.

- Heat oil in a pan and crack some eggs. Cook to your desired doneness, then top with a crown of sauerkraut or kimchi before serving for a fancy spin on eggs. The fermented crunch makes this simple dinner special.

- Cook grains like farro or quinoa, then toss with olive oil, herbs, nuts, and fermented tomatoes or lemons. Their tangy sweetness complements the fluffy grains.

- For plant-based meals, sauté tofu cubes, tempeh, or seitan, then douse in your favorite fermented hot sauce. Balance the heat with a yogurt or tahini dipping sauce. Your tastebuds will tingle.

- Pair rich proteins like steak, pork, and salmon with quick-pickled veggies. Try beets, onions, carrots, or bell peppers for a bright contrast to dense meats.

- Before coating proteins and vegetables, stir miso into veggie or peanut-based salad dressings and marinades. Bake, grill, or pan-fry for added depth of savoriness.

The opportunities to utilize fermented foods at dinnertime are infinite. Incorporate them into balanced meals for amplified nutrition and scrumptious flavors.

Craft Clever Appetizers with Fermented Ingredients

Hosting guests? Impress them with unique appetizers and small plates starring tangy fermented fare.

- Take bruschetta to the next level by topping toasted bread with bean puree, pickled peppers, and olive tapenade rather than plain tomatoes. The mix of flavors and textures excites the palate.

- Serve creamy goat cheese or feta crumbled over crispy fermented rye crackers. The nutty crunch pairs impeccably with the rich, creamy cheese. Add herbs, nuts, or fruit, too.

- Smear crostini or pita crisps with hummus, then top with peppery arugula and pickled red onions for a tangy kick. The light acidity cuts through the chickpea spread.

- Take deviled eggs to new heights by blending mustard, horseradish, or miso into the yolk filling. Garnish with minced quick-pickled veggies for more fermented goodness in each bite.

- Outshine stale crudités and dips by adding sturdy pickled veggies like carrots, radishes, cauliflower, and broccoli. Accompany them with a silky yogurt ranch dip for contrast.

Incorporate fermented ingredients into dips, spreads, toasts, and crostinis for appetizers with visual appeal and addictive tastes. Their sour complexity will excite your guests' palates.

Elevate Desserts with Fermented Fruits

Sweet endings get a tasty, tangy twist when made with live-cultured fruits. Bake them into cakes, compotes, and other naturally sweetened treats.

- Mix fermented berries, chopped dried fruit, and lemon zest into yogurt or cottage cheese for a fast, protein-packed dessert. The tangy berries cut through the richness.

- Blend soaked chia seeds with non-dairy milk and fermented pineapple juice for a dairy-free chia pudding. Top with coconut flakes and lime zest.

- Swirl fermented plum or cherry puree into plain Greek yogurt to create a beautiful parfait. Layer the yogurt with crunchy granola for a contrasting texture.

- Stir chopped preserved lemons, oranges, or grapefruit into muffins, quick bread, or cake batters. Their bright acidity balances the sweetness.

- The next time you crave a pie, make it with a fermented fruit filling, like blueberry, peach, strawberry, or mixed berry. Tangy and sweet is a delightful combination.

Infuse your desserts with sophisticated flavor dimensions by using live-cultured fruits. Their natural sugars caramelize magnificently when baked.

Homemade Condiments with Fermented Flair

Making fermented sauces, relishes, and mustards lets you control the ingredients. You can create great flavors not found in stores.

- Make a spicy fermented hot sauce by blending pickled peppers, like jalapeños, habaneros, or serranos, with spices, garlic, and onion. Then add brine for a sour kick.

- For an addictive fried food topper, whip up kimchi or curtido mayo. Simply fold in chopped fermented cabbage into regular or vegan mayonnaise.

- Add puréed fermented carrots, beets, horseradish, or hot peppers into mustard or mayo to give deviled eggs or grilled meats a kick. Spice it up with extra garlic and herbs.

- Combine pickled ginger with honey, lemon, soy sauce, sesame oil, and ginger for a unique salad dressing. Shake well before drizzling over greens.

- Quick kraut relish can add crunch and tangy sweetness to sandwiches and burgers. Chop sauerkraut with onion and parsley, then dress with oil and vinegar.

Get creative and make your own fermented ketchup, barbecue sauce, ranch dip, salsa, and more. Homemade allows you to control the flavor profile and ingredients.

As you can see, the possibilities for creatively incorporating fermented vegetables into everyday meals are truly endless. Let your imagination run wild. With their unique crunchy textures and tangy tastes, the probiotic power of fermented foods takes any dish from boring to sensational.

Chapter 6: Advanced Fermentation: Expanding Your Skills

Now that you have the basics of vegetable fermentation, you're ready to expand your skills for even tastier and more creative homemade sauerkraut, kimchi, and pickles. In this chapter, you'll level up your fermenting game. First, you'll learn how to experiment with fermenting different vegetables and inventive flavor combos beyond cabbage and cucumbers. You'll discover more about how temperature and time affect fermentation so you can dial in the process to achieve the tastes you love. Lastly, you'll get ideas for transforming your fermented veggies into more elaborate dishes, like tacos, salads, and sandwiches. With the tips in this chapter, you'll gain knowledge and confidence to improvise your imaginative fermented creations while keeping things safe.

11. *Expanding your skills will allow you to ferment more food. Source: Wheeler Cowperthwaite, CC BY 2.0 <https://creativecommons.org/licenses/by/2.0>, via Wikimedia Commons: https://commons.wikimedia.org/wiki/File:Home_fermentation_pr ocess_13.jpg*

Experimenting with Different Vegetables and Combinations

Once you have basic sauerkraut and pickle fermenting under your belt, it's time to experiment with fermenting new vegetables and creative flavor combinations. While cabbage and cucumbers are classic fermenting staples, nearly any vegetable can be fermented through lacto-fermentation. Get ready to explore new dimensions of homemade ferments.

Trying New Vegetables

Many familiar vegetables can be transformed through fermentation. Some additional common vegetables to try fermenting include:

- **Carrots** - Shredded or cut into sticks, carrots become tender with a tangy zip from fermentation. They pair well with ginger, garlic, and lemon. The vibrant orange color brightens any ferment.

- **Cauliflower** - Chopped into florets or thinly sliced, cauliflower ferments excellently. It becomes soft but still retains a pleasant crunch. Echo cauliflower's nutty flavor with cumin and coriander.

- **Broccoli** - Chopped broccoli florets ferment into a tangy and highly nutritious side. Combine broccoli with sliced onions, carrots, and bell peppers for a colorful medley.

- **Green Beans** - Fresh, tender green beans can be left whole or sliced into fermented versions of dilly beans. Add garlic, dill, and hot chilies for extra dimensions.

- **Asparagus** – Asparagus's delicate flavor is nicely accentuated by fermentation. Snap off woody ends and lightly steam before pickling the spears.

- **Turnips** - Thinly sliced or cut into wedges, turnips grow mellower through fermentation. Pair them with beets, garlic, and herbs.

- **Celery** - Chop celery stalks and leaves for a mineral-rich fermented side or condiment. Season with lemon, parsley, and thyme.

- **Radishes** - These spicy root vegetables soften and gain complexity from fermenting. Grate or slice them to combine with daikon, garlic, and ginger.

- **Green Tomatoes** - Unripe green tomatoes sliced thin and fermented develop a tangy flavor. Include spices like black peppercorns, bay leaves, and dried chili.

- **Peppers** - Hot or sweet peppers can be fermented whole, sliced, or diced. Acid brightens their flavors. Try mixing colors and heat levels.

These cover only a handful of the diverse vegetables you can introduce into your fermenting repertoire. Get creative with available seasonal produce in your area. The possibilities are endless.

Crafting Flavorful Brines

While a simple brine of salt and water is essential for fermentation, you can develop more complex flavors through your brining ingredients. Consider adding different elements:

- **Aromatics** - Garlic, onions, shallots, ginger, lemongrass, kaffir lime leaves

- **Herbs** - Dill, basil, cilantro, oregano, marjoram, thyme, rosemary

- **Spices** - Coriander, cumin, fennel, mustard seeds, black pepper, chilies

- **Sweeteners** - Sugar, honey, maple syrup, agave

- **Citrus** - Lemon, lime, grapefruit or orange juice, and zest

- **Vinegar** - Apple cider, coconut, rice wine, red wine, or white wine

- **Umami** - Fish sauce, soy sauce, miso paste, dried mushrooms

12. Herbs can be used in brine to complement the vegetables. Source: https://www.pexels.com/photo/brown-wooden-spoon-with-herbs-on-top-of-green-bamboo-mat-and-brown-wooden-surface-130980/

Use these brine ingredients judiciously to complement the main vegetables instead of overpowering them. Keep vegetable-to-brine ratios balanced and ensure adequate salt for safety. With practice crafting brine, you'll create standout ferments.

Adding Fruits for Flavor and Texture

You can ferment fruits on their own into products like kombucha, fruit leather, or preserved lemons. But small amounts of fruit also lend flavor, acidity, and contrasting texture when combined with vegetables:

- **Apples** - Sliced or grated apples blend well in vegetable ferments. They provide sweetness, tartness, and a pleasant crunch.

- **Grapes** - Halved red or green grapes make a bright, juicy addition to fermented greens or other veggies. The innate antimicrobial properties of grapes can help prolong fermented shelf life.

- **Berries** - Whole raspberries, blueberries, or strawberries lend a burst of summery sweet-tartness and color. Since their skin can trap unwanted yeasts, freeze berries briefly before fermenting.

- **Citrus Fruits** - Thin slices or strips of lemon, lime, orange, or grapefruit contribute vibrant flavor and acidity. Remove visible seeds first.

- **Stone Fruits** - Chopped peaches, plums, apricots, or cherries provide pleasant, sweet accents and a pop of color to fermented mixes.

- **Melons** - Small honeydew, cantaloupe, and watermelon cubes infuse ferments with mild sweetness. Watermelon rind can also be fermented.

Fruits should comprise no more than 10-15% of total vegetable volume to prevent overpowering and keep vegetables properly submerged. But small fruit additions can take ferments to the next level.

Boosting Nutrition with Seeds and Grains

You can introduce more nourishing ingredients into fermented vegetable medleys while enhancing texture:

- **Seeds** - Pepitas, sunflower, chia, and sesame seeds provide healthy fats and crunch. Rinse off salt or seasonings for fermenting.

- **Grains** - Soaked rolled oats, wild rice, quinoa, millet, or amaranth lend wholesome bulk with their nutrition. Rinse grains well.

- **Legumes** - Well-cooked or canned chickpeas, kidney beans, or lentils add plant-based protein. Ensure the beans are softened to avoid deterioration.

- **Nuts** - Slivered or chopped almonds, walnuts, pecans, hazelnuts, or peanuts contribute richness. Presoak to remove tannins.

The key is properly preparing seeds, grains, beans, and nuts before fermenting to avoid undesirable textural changes. Up to 1 cup total volume per 1-quart jar provides ample nutrition without compromising fermentation.

Layering Flavors through Staggered Addition

Instead of adding all produce and seasonings upfront, you can incrementally build flavor:

- Place aromatics like garlic, ginger, and peppers in the bottom of the jar to infuse brines as fermentation begins.

- Start lighter vegetables at the beginning, then add heartier or bitter veggies, like broccoli, cauliflower, or kale, a few days into the ferment after the tanginess develops.

- Sprinkle fresh herbs on top later in the fermentation process so their flavors are retained.

- Add a small amount of whey at the start to acidify and inoculate. Then, incorporate a touch more later to provide bacterial reinforcement without excessive acidity.

This technique creates more complex, multi-layered flavor profiles. However, ensure to pack new ingredient additions tightly and monitor overall brine levels.

Creating Your Signature Concoctions

Once you understand basic principles, the possibilities for conjuring your fermented vegetable medleys are endless. Consider:

- **Regional Themes** - Create Indian-inspired mixes of cauliflower, golden raisins, and curry spices. Or opt for an Italian blend of bell peppers, garlic, basil, and oregano.

- **Dietary Themes** - Craft vegan kimchis with radish, lemongrass, and ginger. Or a probiotic-rich vegetarian Tex-Mex with tomatillos, jalapeños, and cumin.

- **Seasonal Themes** - Highlight summer's bounty with zucchini, tomatoes, and cilantro. Or showcase root veggies in autumnal batches of beets, parsnips, and caraway.

- **Color Themes** - Build visual appeal through contrasting hues by fermenting purple cabbage with orange carrots and yellow peppers.

Taste test batches of creative combinations. Make notes on successes to recreate. Keep a list of ingredient amounts and ratios as you improvise your signature fermented vegetable medleys.

Probiotic Pickled Salad

Take your fermentation skills to the next level by turning chopped pickled vegetables into a zesty probiotic salad.

Ingredients:

- 1 cup shredded red cabbage

- 1 cup sliced cucumbers

- ½ cup diced red onion

- ½ cup chopped dill pickle

- ¼ cup diced jalapeño

- 1 clove garlic, minced

- 1 tbsp. apple cider vinegar

- 1 tsp. mustard seeds

- ½ tsp. salt

  - Fresh dill for garnish

Instructions

1. Wash and prepare vegetables. Place shredded cabbage and cucumber slices into a 1-quart mason jar.

2. Add onion, pickled cucumber, jalapeño, and garlic on top. Pour vinegar and 1 cup water over the vegetables.

3. Add mustard seeds and salt. Seal the jar and ferment for 3-5 days.

4. Once sufficiently sour, drain the brine from the vegetables. Add fresh dill. Serves 4.

Get creative with fermented salad blends using seasonal produce and favorite spices. Adjust the brine strength and fermenting time to achieve your preferred tanginess.

With an understanding of basic principles, you can craft any vegetable into tasty homemade ferments. Start simple, then get adventurous by combining your fermented creations with fruits, aromatics, and culinary influences from around the world. Fermentation opens up an unlimited world of possibilities for creating signature probiotic-powered condiments and sides to enliven any meal.

Understanding the Role of Temperature and Time

Mastering the nuances of how temperature and time impact fermentation lets you fine-tune the process for your ideal tastes and textures. Minor adjustments make a big difference in the finished products. Here are detailed temperature and time guidelines so you can confidently control fermentation.

Importance of Temperature

Temperature significantly influences vegetable fermentation in several ways. It determines fermentation speed, with warmer temperatures accelerating microbial activity and fermentation, while cooler temperatures slow it down. Temperature also affects texture, as too cold can halt fermentation before vegetables fully break down, while too warm can cause undesirably soft vegetables. Temperature impacts microbial populations since different bacteria thrive at different temperature ranges. The ideal veggie lactic acid fermentation range is 60-75°F. Below 50°F fermentation stalls, and above 80°F, ferments may spoil.

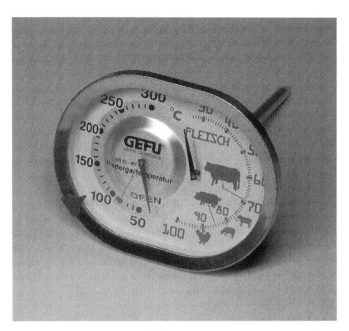

13. Temperature significantly influences vegetable fermentation.
Source: Rainer Z ..., CC BY-SA 3.0
<https://creativecommons.org/licenses/by-sa/3.0>, via Wikimedia
Commons:
https://commons.wikimedia.org/wiki/File:Bratenthermometer-
1.jpg

Additionally, temperature changes flavor profiles, with cooler temperatures leading to slower, more complex flavor development, while warmer temperatures quickly create sourness. Temperature can encourage contamination, as temperatures above 80°F provide the opportunity for yeasts and molds to establish before desired bacteria take hold. Lastly, temperature helps determine safety since at 50-120°F, lactic acid bacteria outcompete pathogens. But outside that range, risks increase. Controlling ambient fermentation temperature gives you leverage to achieve the intended results.

Monitoring Temperature

When fermenting vegetables, you can monitor temperatures using several methods. A fermentation chamber or sous vide setup maintains the desired temperature. Placing a liquid thermometer into the fermenting jar tracks internal temperature. Fermentation coolers filled with water automatically maintain temperatures under 80°F. Household spaces like a pantry, kitchen, or basement that stay naturally in the 60-75°F range also work.

Outdoor spaces like shade in warm months or burying vessels in the soil to stabilize temperature are an option. If it's too cold, heating pads or rice socks can gently warm jars when wrapped around them to prevent overheating. Refrigeration cools batches that are fermenting too rapidly. Observe temperature trends over days, adjusting placements or heating and cooling accordingly. Ideal consistent temperature encourages the best fermentation.

Warm Temperature Fermentation

In warmer temperature ranges, around 68-78°F, you can expect faster fermentation. Vegetables ferment and soften more quickly, within 5-7 days. Rapid acidification happens as bacteria generate lactic acid faster. More straightforward flavors result without time for complexity, with dominant sour, tangy notes coming through. Closer monitoring is required to avoid over-softening or spoilage. Smaller batches ferment more evenly than larger amounts in heat. Warm temperatures demand vigilance but allow quick results. This temperature range works well in most indoor kitchens or heated outdoor setups.

Cool Temperature Fermentation

With cooler temperature fermentation around 60-65°F, the process requires more time, typically 2-3 weeks. Slower acidification provides an opportunity for more nuanced flavors to emerge. Vegetables retain crunchiness rather than softening. Lower temperatures favor more diversity in microbial populations beyond only main lactic acid bacteria. Contamination risks are reduced compared to warmer fermentation. While harnessing cooler temperatures brings benefits, you need patience. Use cellars, fermentation coolers, or monitor refrigeration to achieve these temperatures.

Variable Temperature Fermentation

Temperature fluctuations during fermentation create challenges. Microbes may struggle to thrive if shifted significantly above or below their ideal range. Inconsistent temperatures can lead to textural irregularities within the same batch, with some spots fermenting more than others. Stalled fermentation may happen if temperatures drop too low, as portions exposed to the coolest spots stop fermenting entirely. Higher temperatures later in the fermentation can cause undesirably soft vegetables as cell walls degrade. Flavor outcomes become less predictable without steady conditions for microbial activity. If temperature bounces up and down, fermentation can still succeed but requires extra vigilance, so minimize fluctuations.

Tips for Dialing in Temperature

Implement temperature control tactics to achieve your intended results. Match vessels and ingredients to conditions using smaller batches for variable temps and fermenting in a glass during cool weather versus crocks in warm conditions.

Move vessels to warmer or cooler spots as needed to maintain desired temperatures. Wrap or uncover jars to modulate heat by insulating them with towels if too cold or uncovering if too warm.

Use water or soil's stable temperature by partially burying jars underground or immersing them in water baths for steady temps. Employ heating or cooling devices cautiously, wrapping hot pads or cold packs to avoid overshooting intended temperatures. Adapt processes to conditions by accepting slower fermentation in cool weather or less acidity if warmer. You can accommodate varied temperatures for successful fermentation year-round with attentive monitoring and adjustment.

How Time Impacts Fermentation

In addition to temperature, the element of time significantly influences fermentation. Time determines the degree of acidification, as more time allows lactic acid levels to increase, lowering pH. It affects texture changes like softening, with shorter ferments leading to crunchier vegetables. Time enables more complex flavor transformations beyond sourness to develop. It makes ferments more strongly preservative at pH levels that inhibit pathogens.

Extended time can encourage contamination if ferments aren't quickly acidified, as prolonged exposure risks mold. Time allows the full enzymatic breakdown of fibers like pectin for texture changes. It impacts microbial diversity, as some bacteria only emerge later into longer fermentations. Managing duration in tandem with temperature gives you complete control over the fermentation process.

Short Term Fermentation

For mild, quick pickles and accelerated fermentation, ferment for 2-5 days if temperatures are in the warmer 68°F+ range. Expect primarily leuconostoc bacterial activity and more restrained acidity. Vegetable texture remains fairly crunchy without extensive breakdown. Basic sour flavor predominates without complexity from long transforms. Lower acidity means these quick pickles require refrigeration to stop fermentation. With attentive chilling, even brief fermentation imparts light pickled flavor and preservative qualities.

Medium Term Fermentation

The 1-3 week duration used for common vegetable fermentation allows dominance of lactobacilli bacteria with moderate acid level development as pH lowers. Softening of vegetable textures occurs as the cell walls break down through enzymatic action. Time enables more complex aromas to emerge, although the flavor is still primarily tangy. Adequate acidity develops for short-term room temperature preservation once fermenting ceases. This 1-3 week timeframe suits most common vegetable ferments, like sauerkraut and dilly beans.

Extended Fermentation

Allowing fermentation to proceed for over 1 month produces more intensely transformed results. pH steadily drops below 4.0 as lactic acid bacteria continue producing acids, making ferments highly preservative. Vegetable textures become extremely soft or mushy as enzymatic action and acids degrade cell structure. Flavor profiles grow increasingly complex with the emergence of subtle fruity, roasted, cheesy, floral, or earthy notes.

The diversity of microbial populations also expands over time. However, risks of contamination and spoilage grow over prolonged exposure if processes aren't pristinely managed. Extended fermentation concentrates flavors and preservative attributes but requires meticulous technique. The slowness also allows unique bacteria to contribute.

Modifying Processing Times

You can adjust your procedures to fine-tune fermentation durations. To slow fermentation, use refrigeration, larger batches, and higher salt levels. Use warmer temperatures, smaller batches, and moderate salt concentrations to accelerate the process. You can pause acid development at the desired stage by rapidly chilling containers, which inhibits microbial activity. Transferring ferments to smaller containers eliminates oxygen, allowing fermentation to continue.

Regularly checking progress lets you shift vessels to warmer or cooler temperatures to speed up or slow down fermentation. You can calibrate fermentation times perfectly for individual tastes and ingredients with attentive monitoring and willingness to intervene.

Achieving Prime Texture

Managing time impacts the textures achieved through fermentation. For crunchy vegetables, opt for brief 1-3 day ferments, refrigerate quickly to halt softening enzymatic action, and use higher salt levels. For firm-tender vegetables, allow 1-2 weeks for the partial breakdown of fibers, and use moderate salt and cool temperatures to slow softening. For tender vegetables, permit 3-4 weeks of fermentation to fully soften cell structures through enzymatic processes, with warmer temperatures encouraging softness. For mushy vegetables, allow over 4 weeks warmer temperatures, limited salt, extended enzymatic action, and acid hydrolysis to weaken vegetable fibers. The time and conditions you allow for fermentation determine the resulting textures based on your preferences.

Preventing Spoilage

Time factors into spoilage prevention. Rapidly acidifying vegetables through warmer temperature fermentation and added lactic acid cultures inhibits mold and yeasts before they take hold. Optimal fermentation times minimize risk, as too short raises the pH enough to risk spoilage, while too long allows contamination. Once sufficiently fermented, bottling reduces risks of airborne yeasts or molds establishing themselves over long open-vessel timeframes. Avoiding exceedingly large batches that take longer to penetrate with inhibitory acidity compared to smaller amounts is wise. With appropriately managed timeframes, you can guide your ferments to perfect acidity before contamination risks heighten.

Understanding time and temperature variables allows you to calibrate fermentation to suit your tastes, textures, schedules, and conditions. Monitor your processes and adjust these factors to achieve optimal pickles, kraut, kimchi, and other fermented delights every time.

Creating Complex Fermented Vegetable Dishes

Making fermented vegetables can add lots of flavor to your meals. Basic ferments like sauerkraut and kimchi are pretty easy to make. But you can create more complex and interesting fermented veggie dishes with some creativity.

Here's how to make fermented vegetable medleys, flavorful sauces, and decorative ferments that look like art.

Root Vegetable Medley

Combining veggies creates cool colors and textures and unique tastes. Here's a recipe for a root veggie ferment medley.

Ingredients:

- 1 cup shredded carrots

- 1 cup shredded beets

- 1 cup shredded turnips

- 1 cup shredded radishes

- 1/2 cup thinly sliced onion

- 2 cloves minced garlic

- 1 tbsp. sea salt

- 4 cups water

Instructions:

1. Mix all the veggies, garlic, and salt in a big bowl. Squish and massage them together so the salt makes them release liquid. This kickstarts fermentation.

2. Pack the mix tightly into a 1-quart jar, pushing down hard to get rid of air pockets. Leave at least 1 inch of space at the top.

3. Make a brine by stirring 2 tbsp. salt into the 4 cups water. Pour this over the veggies to cover them completely.

4. Seal the jar tightly and let it ferment at room temp for 2 to 4 weeks. Then, store in the fridge for up to 6 months.

Mix up other veggie combos in your ferments, too. The options are endless for tasty medleys.

Italian Medley

You can boost flavor with aromatic ingredients, like garlic, onions, herbs, and spices. Here's a recipe for an Italian-tasting fermented veggie blend.

Ingredients:

- 2 cups sliced zucchini
- 1 cup halved cherry tomatoes
- 1 jalapeno, sliced
- 4 cloves minced garlic
- 2 tbsp. dried oregano
- 1/4 cup chopped basil
- 1/4 cup halved black olives
- 1 tbsp. sea salt
- 2 cups water

Instructions:

1. Mix the veggies, garlic, oregano, olives, and salt in a bowl. Squish together so the salt pulls the liquid out.

2. Firmly pack the mix into a 1-quart jar, pressing down hard to remove air pockets.

3. Pour the brine (2 cups water + 1 tbsp. salt) over the veggies to cover them.

4. Seal the jar and let it ferment at room temp for 3 to 5 weeks.

5. Once fermented, stir in the fresh basil. Store in the fridge.

Swap in your favorite aromatic veggies and herbs. Get creative with global flavor combos.

Cherry Pepper Ferment

You can add fruits and edible flowers for natural sweetness. Here's a recipe for a cherry pepper ferment.

Ingredients:

- 1 lb. sliced assorted hot peppers
- 1 cup halved cherry tomatoes
- 1/2 cup pitted and halved cherries
- 1 tbsp. chopped dill
- 1 tbsp. sea salt
- 2 cups water

Instructions:

1. Mix the peppers, tomatoes, cherries, dill, and salt in a bowl. Squish together so the salt pulls the liquid out.

2. Firmly pack the mix into a 1-quart jar, pressing down hard to remove air pockets.

3. Pour the brine (2 cups water + 1 tbsp. salt) over to cover completely.

4. Seal the jar and let it ferment at room temp for 2 to 4 weeks.

5. Once fermented, store in the fridge for up to 6 months. Use as a condiment, salsa, or topping.

The natural sugar in fruit goes great with the salty, tangy flavor of fermented veggies. Try your sweet-savory combo ideas.

Romesco Sauce

Blend up brine-rich veggies into flavorful sauces and spreads. Here's a recipe for Romesco sauce:

Ingredients:

- 1 cup chopped fermented bell peppers
- 1/4 cup toasted almonds
- 2 cloves garlic, chopped
- 1 tbsp. sherry vinegar
- 1/4 cup olive oil
- Salt to taste

Instructions:

1. Blend the peppers, almonds, garlic, vinegar, and olive oil in a food processor until smooth.

2. Add salt to taste. The brine from the peppers should make it salty enough already.

3. Store the sauce in an airtight container in the fridge for up to 2 months.

4. Use as a flavorful sauce for fish, chicken, veggies, and sandwiches.

Let your creativity run wild, creating tasty, fermented veggie sauces and spreads.

Skewered Cauliflower Ferment

You can make decorative ferments that look like edible art. Here's an idea for skewered cauliflower ferments.

Ingredients:

- 1 head cauliflower, cut into florets
- 4 wooden skewers soaked in water
- 1 tbsp. fresh grated turmeric
- 1 tsp. mustard seeds
- 1 tsp. chili flakes
- 1 tbsp. sea salt
- 2 cups water

Instructions:

1. Toss the cauliflower florets with the turmeric, mustard seeds, chili flakes, and salt. Massage in the spices.

2. Thread the spiced florets onto the soaked wooden skewers, leaving 1/2-inch gaps between pieces.

3. Place the skewers in a container and pour the brine (2 cups water + 1 tbsp. salt) over to cover completely.

4. Let it ferment at room temp for 5 to 7 days. Once fermented, store the skewers submerged in brine in the fridge for up to 3 months.

Make your fermented veggies look as awesome as they taste. Stack, stuff, layer, and skewer them for a pretty presentation.

Fermenting veggies doesn't have to be boring. Use creative combinations, flavors, fruits, and designs to make complex and amazing fermented vegetable dishes. The fermenting process stays the same—salt the veggies to draw out moisture, pack them tightly to remove air, cover them with brine, and ferment them for 2 to 6 weeks.

Let your imagination run wild with ingredients and visuals. With these tips, you should feel inspired to create your signature complex veggie ferments that look and taste incredible.

Chapter 7: Troubleshooting and Common Issues

When fermenting foods at home, you will face challenges along the way. Don't panic. With a little troubleshooting, you can get your ferments back on track. This chapter teaches you how to tackle mold and other unwanted microbes that may grow in your ferments. You'll uncover techniques for tweaking flavors and textures if your sauerkraut, kimchi, or other fermented foods aren't panning out quite right. Most importantly, you'll get pointers for rescuing batches that have become over or under-fermented. With the proper information and a bit of patience, you can beat the most frequent hurdles in fermentation. Heed the guidance in this chapter, and you'll steadily churn out flavorful, wholesome ferments.

14. Mold is a challenge you can face when fermenting food. Source: Ganesh Mohan T, CC BY-SA 4.0 <https://creativecommons.org/licenses/by-sa/4.0>, via Wikimedia Commons: https://commons.wikimedia.org/wiki/File:Mold_growing_in_Goo seberry.jpg

Addressing Mold and Undesirable Microorganisms

When fermenting vegetables, avoiding contamination by molds with other undesirable microorganisms that can spoil batches is imperative. By understanding what encourages these organisms and implementing preventive practices, you can consistently craft reliable, delicious, and safe homemade ferments.

What Causes Mold in Fermented Foods?

Mold growth during fermentation happens due to several factors. Exposure to oxygen enables aerobic molds to thrive. Keeping vegetables submerged beneath brine is critical to avoiding oxygen. Any pieces breaching the brine surface are vulnerable. Weights help keep vegetables immersed. Low acidity provides insufficient inhibition of molds. Achieving a pH at or below 4.6 through lactic acid fermentation deters most molds. Faster acidification protects against mold establishment.

Ambient spores landing on exposed vegetable surfaces or brines can proliferate if conditions are ideal. Airborne mold spores are ubiquitous. Hence, covering vessels limits exposure. Limited microbial competition leaves room for mold growth. Inoculating brines with lactic acid bacteria crowds out undesirables. Warm temperatures accelerate mold growth.

Ideal vegetable fermentation temperatures below 75°F limit mold risks. High humidity encourages mold, while dry conditions deter it. Keeping fermentation vessel lids on maintains carbon dioxide saturation, which suppresses mold. With mindful practices, you can prevent circumstances allowing mold footholds during fermentation. But if uncontrolled, mold can quickly proliferate.

Identifying Mold

Recognizing mold visibility is vital to early intervention. White mold in the form of powdery white filaments on the brine surface is common. The mold Rhizopus oligosporus frequently occurs. It indicates oxygen has reached the brine.

Fuzzy patches may form on exposed vegetables or sides of vessels. These signal higher humidity and airborne spores. On prolonged exposure to air, white molds may develop blue, green, black, or pink hues indicating sporulation.

Slimy yellow or brownish deposits result from yeast-like Aureobasidium mold. While molds can initially appear harmless as thin white layers, they quickly release spores and expand if not promptly removed at first signs. Routinely checking for growth is essential.

Preventing Mold before Starting Fermentation

You can take front-end measures to avoid mold during fermentation. Sanitize all equipment with vinegar, boiling water, or bleach solution to destroy residual spores from prior batches. Wash vegetables thoroughly before fermenting. Scrub skins and remove damaged or bruised portions that could harbor unseen molds. Pack vegetables tightly into jars, pressing out air pockets, and maintain brine coverage. Don't overfill containers initially.

Ensure sufficient salt concentrations and fast acid development using whey or starter culture inoculants that drop pH quickly. Use airlock lids or tighten regular lids to limit air exchange. Avoid reused commercial pickle lids with compromised seals. Keep fermentation vessels away from high-humidity areas, like dishwashers or sinks. Avoid temperature fluctuations that cause condensation. With clean, sanitized gear and attentive vegetable preparation, you remove potential mold sources before beginning fermentation.

Ongoing Mold Prevention

Once fermenting, maintain vegetables below brine level by weighing them down to keep them submerged. Top off brine if any are exposed. Check vessels daily for signs of surface growth and remove them promptly since mold can establish rapidly. Avoid unnecessarily opening containers by using an airlock lid or opening briefly to "burp" gases, then resealing. Keep fermentation vessels away from direct sunlight, as ultraviolet light can generate mold-inhibiting hydrogen peroxide in brine.

Regularly wipe away moisture that condenses on lids or container sides using a clean cloth dipped in vinegar. Remove whole spices with a sterile tool once they impart flavor, as they can eventually harbor molds. You can prevent mold from gaining a foothold with constant vigilance and immediate correction of risky circumstances.

Fixing Minor Surface Mold

If a small amount of mold forms, promptly skim off only the mold using a clean utensil and discard. Avoid stirring up spores unnecessarily. Spray vinegar on the problem area and wipe with a clean cloth, as vinegar further inhibits mold regrowth. Check the vegetables are still submerged, weighing them back down under brine if any floated into the danger zone. Taste a sample. If it has a normal tangy acidic flavor without off-tastes, the unaffected batch can be safely fermented. Catching minor surface mold early and quickly rectifying conditions can often salvage the batch. But extensive mold requires discarding.

Dealing with Significant Mold

If mold spreads substantially before detection, do not consume moldy fermented vegetables, as mold can impart off flavors and potentially liberate toxins. Discard entire batches with colored mold growing within vegetables or brine as the tendrils penetrate surrounding food. Clean containers with interior mold thoroughly using vinegar, soap, and bleach solution before reusing. Review processes to identify adjustments to prevent repeat issues, like increasing inoculants, lowering pH faster, and eliminating oxygen. While disheartening, tossing bad batches removes risks. Only minimal surface mold is fixable. Learn from mistakes.

Preventing Other Problematic Microbes

In addition to molds, a few other microorganisms can occasionally cause issues. Kahm yeast leaves a film atop brines and alters flavor with fruity, fermenting notes. It indicates exposure to oxygen. Promptly skim off the growth you spot and prevent further air entry. Lactobacillus brevis can generate "ropy" slime that makes brines viscous. It's harmless but unappealing. Selecting the right starter cultures inhibits ropy strains. If slime develops, gently stir to redistribute the brine.

Gas-forming coliforms produce excess gas, making ferments carbonated and causing off odors. Using starter cultures avoids coliform growth. If bubbles form, you can stir gently to release trapped gases. With good practices, unwanted microbes rarely become problematic. But quickly addressing issues when they arise helps avoid losing batches.

Troubleshooting Environmental Factors

If battling persistent mold or other microbes, reexamine your overall fermentation environment. Is the space prone to high humidity and temperature swings? Try a cooler, dryer area less susceptible to condensation-triggering mold. Does the ambient air harbor mold spores? Improve ventilation and add a dehumidifier. Avoid fermenting adjacent to compost bins or grass piles.

Are small fruit flies or gnats present? They can carry spores. Set up fly traps and keep produce covered pre-fermentation. Is the kitchen ventilation poor? Steam, frying, and humid air contribute to moisture. Cover vessels but increase kitchen airflow. While microbes directly cause spoilage, reassessing the surrounding conditions provides clues for creating an overall fermentation-friendly space. Adjusting external factors alleviates contamination risks.

Using Mold Inhibitors

You can add natural mold-inhibiting compounds to discourage growth. A pinch of powdered citric acid added to brine quickly acidifies, inhibiting mold with minimal flavor impact. Adding a tablespoon of vinegar to brine acidifies faster while preventing mold, without altering the color. Rinsed grape leaves contribute antimicrobial compounds that help limit mold growth. Place one atop vegetables before brine.

Garlic's antifungal allicin can hinder mold. Add 2-3 cloves of crushed garlic to the brine. Spices like cinnamon, cloves, black pepper, and chili flakes have antifungal properties. Add 1/2 tsp. of one per pint jar. With a light hand, these pantry items help tilt fermentation conditions against mold establishment without overwhelming flavor.

Adopting Reliable Recipes

The ingredients and methods specified in recipes greatly impact results. Trust recipes from reputable scientific or traditional sources over dubious online recipes with scant details or safety information. Avoid adding thickeners like xanthan gum, which increases risks. Follow traditional combinations and proportions. Compare multiple recipes and select ones favoring salt levels on the higher end of the safe 2-5% range, which impedes mold growth.

Prioritize recipes using pH meters over approximate timeframes for determining doneness. Relying on objective pH measurements prevents prematurely halting fermentation before adequate acidity develops. Starting with well-vetted, science-based recipes removes guesswork and uncertainty undermining success and safety.

Knowing When to Toss Bad Batches

With attention and prevention efforts, you can avoid most mold situations. But if a batch does go south, discard ferment showing colored mold interiors, as erring on the side of caution protects health. Toss batches with off odors, textures, or profuse bubbling indicating yeasts or coliforms. Don't second-guess your instincts. If mold reappears repeatedly despite sanitizing, reexamine your entire process and fermentation space. Avoid tasting or cooking risky ferments, as heat does not destroy mycotoxins from molds.

Though it stings to waste time and ingredients, embracing a better-safe-than-sorry mentality keeps your homemade ferments reliably delicious and wholesome.

By understanding what encourages mold and spoilage while proactively managing fermentation conditions, you guide the process to yield abundant lactic acid and avoid circumventing contamination pitfalls reliably. With observation and care, your fermented vegetables will develop complex flavors free from off notes or textural flaws batch after batch. Don't let sporadic mold dissuade you. Correct missteps and fill your pantry with nourishing ferments.

Adjusting Flavors and Textures during Fermentation

One of the joys of fermenting vegetables is experimenting to develop your ideal flavors and textures. Knowing how ingredients and processes influence outcomes, you can calibrate each batch to achieve customizable results that perfectly suit your taste. This section explores adjustments to target tanginess, sourness, crunch, and other traits in your fermented creations.

Balancing Acidity

The acidity level significantly impacts flavor and preservation potential. Acidity arises as lactic acid bacteria convert sugars to lactic acid, lowering pH. Too little acidity risks spoilage, while too many tastes overly sour. Boost acidity by adding whey or starter culture, fermenting at warmer temperatures around 70°F, using lower salt levels, and fermenting for longer durations. To limit acidity, ferment at cooler 60-65°F temperatures, use higher salt concentrations of up to 5%, and check progress early before extensive sourness develops.

Monitor acidity using pH strips or meters. Your target is a final pH of 3.3-3.8 acidity for a tangy yet balanced flavor. You will calibrate techniques to achieve your ideal flavors and food safety acidity with experience.

Influencing Sourness

Sourness depends on lactic acid but also acetic acid. Lactic acid provides a rounded, mellow sourness. Acetic acid has a sharp, vinegary bite. You can encourage lactic acid production through optimal fermentation conditions for lactic acid bacteria. Limit oxygen exposure, which enables acetic acid bacteria responsible for acetic acid to eliminate headspace when jarring. If the sourness is too sharp, gently boil fermented vegetables to drive off some acetic acid.

Blend in a small amount of sweetness using minced fruit, fruit juice, or a pinch of sugar to balance sourness. Managing the two main acids lets you customize the nuances of sourness in ferments.

Adjusting Salty Flavors

Since salt is vital for safety, don't alter concentrations too drastically. But you can fine-tune saltiness. Use the lower range of recommended salt percentages for a less salty flavor, around 2% of the vegetable weight. For pronounced saltiness, go up to 5% salt by weight, recognizing this slows fermentation. After primary fermentation, you can briefly soak vegetables to leach out some overt saltiness before serving. If saltiness is lacking, add a sprinkling of mineral salt on top before transferring it to storage.

Add salty accent flavors through sauerkraut seasonings, like caraway seeds, celery seeds, or dill. By staying within safe guidelines, salt adjustments provide flexibility to calibrate to taste.

Managing Spicy Heat

The piquancy of fermented foods depends on ingredients and methods. Hot peppers contain capsaicin and related compounds that add spicy heat. Select peppers based on Scoville units indicating relative spiciness. Slice peppers thinly and add judiciously to allow their heat to diffuse during fermentation. Prevent hot spices from scorching other ingredients by enclosing them in cheesecloth satchels.

If desiring less heat, substitute sweet bell peppers or use a mixture of hot and sweet. Or add peppers later into the ferment rather than initially. Allowing long fermentation durations mellows capsaicin heat through enzymatic processes. You can create pleasantly piquant fermented condiments with strategic pepper selection and restrained use.

Balancing Sweetness

Minimal sweetness balances and rounds out acidity. Options for adding subtly sweet notes include grating in a small amount of carrot, apple, pear, or beet, but limit to 1 cup per 1-quart jar, as too much sugar fuels yeasts. Add a pinch of natural sugar or maple syrup, starting with 1/4 tsp. per pint jar and adjusting to taste. Mixing in a few raisins, currants, chopped prunes, or dried cranberries contributes concentrated sweetness.

Including a thin, sweet onion slice or shallot is another option, as onion sugars break down during fermentation. Toward the end, blending in a few fresh herb leaves, like mint, basil, or lemon balm, provides delicate, sweet brightness. You can craft balanced complexity with restrained use of fruits, vegetables, or sugars.

Lowering Sodium

For those limiting sodium, marginally reducing salt can help. Use 2% salt by weight, the lowest safe amount for fermentation, to lower sodium versus higher percentages. Substitute a portion of salt with potassium chloride salt substitute, though excess potassium chloride can cause bitterness. After primary fermentation, rinse vegetables in cool water to leach out surface sodium, if tolerable to flavor. Pair fermented foods with fresh vegetables, fruits, whole grains, and lean proteins to reduce overall dietary sodium. While fermented foods promote health, these strategies moderately decrease sodium content.

Adjusting Texture

The techniques determine the resulting texture. For softer vegetables, ferment at warmer temperatures, around 70°F, until fully tenderized by acids. Allowing fermentation to proceed for over 2 weeks softens vegetables through enzymatic breakdown of pectins in cell walls. Firmer textures result from cooler fermentation temperatures around 60-64°F and limiting time to under 1 week.

Adding higher salt concentrations up to 5% helps maintain crispness by inhibiting softening enzymes. Refrigerating early into fermentation halts softening by slowing veggie enzymes and bacteria. You can achieve crunchy, crisp-tender, or soft vegetables through strategic process timing and temperature control.

Troubleshooting Textural Problems

If undesirable textures result, mushy vegetables can indicate allowing fermentation to progress too long, so try shorter durations. If still too soft, increase salt levels slightly within a safe range to slow softening enzymes. For ferments that remain crunchier than desired, allow more time for acid hydrolysis of pectins to tenderize. Check recipes for errors like inaccurate salt measurements altering outcomes. Pay attention to textures and adjust subsequent batches to achieve your perfect level of crispy versus tenderized vegetables.

Preventing Ropiness

Occasionally, a "ropy" or viscous texture results from specific bacteria. Certain strains of Lactobacillus cause a polysaccharide sliminess termed ropiness. It is safe but unappealing. Selecting the right starter cultures prevents ropy strains from dominating. Inoculate brine upfront with anti-rope strains. If slime forms, stir gently to redistribute. Transferring to a clean jar might help. Limit oxygen exposure. Check overall fermentation conditions, as ropiness can signal overly warm temperatures or another issue. While harmless, ropiness is unappetizing. Carefully chosen cultures and attentive fermentation help avoid it.

Troubleshooting Unpleasant Flavors

If off or strongly unpleasant flavors occur, assess overall fermentation duration and temperature, as flaws often trace to extremes in time or temperature that hinder good bacteria. Off odors may indicate contamination by yeasts or mold, so examine closely for signs and discard the batch if compromised. Bitterness can arise from letting fermentation progress excessively long or from incorrect starter culture strains.

If overly vinegary, acetic acid bacteria may have dominated, so use gentler heating to drive off some acetic acid. For putrid flavors, closely review sanitation and preparation practices to identify required improvements. When flavors seem off, examine your processes to pinpoint likely causes and make appropriate adjustments.

Masking Flaws

If slightly "off" flavors occur in an otherwise safe batch, you can mix in fresh diced aromatics, like onion, peppers, carrots, or herbs, to mask subtle off notes, as their flavors will dominate. Blend the slightly flawed ferment with a new, correctly fermented batch to dilute odd flavors.

Pair the ferment with strongly flavored foods, like curries, BBQ, or Caesar dressing, so flaws recede. If appearance allows, puree or chop fermented vegetables into dips or sauces to integrate off-tastes. By being creative, you can salvage somewhat imperfect ferments. But serious flaws require discarding.

By manipulating ingredients, duration, temperature, and techniques, you can modify acidity, saltiness, spice, sweetness, texture, and other traits in ferments. Adjust one variable at a time, making notes. You will hone processes for ferments precisely matched to your unique tastes with experimentation.

Tips for Salvaging Over-Fermented or Under-Fermented Batches

Even experienced fermenters occasionally end up with suboptimal results like under or over-fermented vegetables. But don't despair. Here are approaches for salvaging, masking flaws, repurposing, and learning from imperfect ferments. With resourcefulness, many batches can still be redeemed.

Identifying Under-Fermented Vegetables

Under-fermented vegetables result from inadequate bacterial activity and acid production. Signs include a crunchy or unsoftened texture since cell walls haven't broken down through acid hydrolysis. There is a mild or lacking sour flavor because the pH remains too high. Cloudy brine signals insufficient lactic acid bacteria growth. Incomplete curing means insufficient preservative effects. Slow bubbling or lack of carbon dioxide release indicates fermentation is stalling. Catching under-fermentation early maximizes options for correction. Taste and observe closely as the process unfolds.

Causes of Under-Fermentation

Under-fermentation typically stems from the temperature being too low to enable lactic acid bacteria since fermentation stalls below 50°F. Insufficient starter culture or lactic acid bacteria can slow acidification. Low salt content fails to inhibit undesirable microbes competing with LAB. Not enough sugars prevent fermenting microbes from metabolizing into acids.

Contamination by undesirable yeasts, mold, or other microorganisms is another cause. Insufficient brine submersion allows oxygen entry and aerobic surface mold. Air entering vessels mid-process suppresses anaerobic fermentation. By identifying likely causes, you can make corrections and get fermentation back on track.

How to Rescue Under-Fermented Batches

To complete fermentation that's too slow, under-acidified, and lacking preservative effects, transfer jars to a warm spot at 60-75°F to restart fermentation, monitoring closely. Add a tablespoon of whey from finished kraut or other fermented vegetables as a starter culture to each jar and stir gently. If fermentation was initiated with inadequate salt, add extra within safe parameters.

If the vegetables become exposed, re-press them to release more brine, and add reserved initial brine as needed. For mixtures lacking sugars, sprinkle a pinch or two of sugar over the top to fuel further fermentation. With TLC and minor additions, you can often get a languishing ferment to pick up again.

Preventing Under-Fermented Spoilage

While reviving an under-fermented batch, be alert for signs of spoilage. Discard the batch if mold is present, as mold spreads rapidly through acid-deficient brine. Don't take risks. Check for ropy and slimy consistency, signaling that undesirable bacteria outpaced lactic acid producers. Off odors of putrefaction, ammonia, yeast, or fermenting suggest the batch has spoiled. When in doubt, don't consume. A ferment that fails to sufficiently acidify promptly is prone to growing problematic microorganisms.

Masking Under-Fermented Flaws

If a batch retains subtle off-flavors once supplemental fermentation is complete, you can mix it into a fresh, correctly fermented batch to dilute slight defects. Pair it with pungent foods like chili sauce, curry, or vinaigrette to cover up flavor issues. Puree it into a dip with herbs and spices to disguise imperfections. With creativity, you can make the best of slightly funny ferments unfit for straight-up eating.

Learning from Under-Fermentation Issues

Make notes to improve the next attempts if under-fermentation recurs. Examine the entire process for missteps like low starter culture or insufficient salt that needs correcting. Look critically at the recipe. If there are repeated issues, compare other recipes to identify potential flaws. Consider environmental factors and maintain more stable warmer temperatures. Increase ventilation. Improve sanitation to avoid batches contaminated with yeasts or mold before lactic acid takes hold. Every batch offers lessons. Strive to determine root causes rather than repeating errors.

Identifying Over-Fermented Vegetables

On the flip side, over-fermentation creates challenges. Soft, mushy texture results from too much acid hydrolysis and pectin breakdown. There is a very pronounced sour flavor and high acidity from extensive fermentation. Darkening colors occur as pigments and antioxidants degrade. Possible off-flavors like bitterness arise from excessive amino acid breakdown. Small bubbles or pockets in the product signal overactive fermentation. Catch over-fermentation early before quality declines too far by tasting and checking texture frequently.

Causes of Over-Fermentation

The main variables provoking over-fermentation include excessive time beyond optimal fermentation ranges, high ambient temperatures accelerating acidification, inadequate salt concentrations enabling runaway microbial activity, and low vegetable-to-brine ratio limiting ability to absorb acids. Allowing pH to drop excessively low, well under 4.0 also over-ferments. Once conditions pass ideal thresholds for your ingredients, rapid quality deterioration results.

Reigning in Runaway Ferments

If you catch over-fermentation shortly after it surpasses prime, refrigerate immediately to suspend microbial activity and acid production. Transfer to smaller sealed containers to minimize headspace and oxygen. If flavors seem dull or flat, add a pinch of sugar to stimulate flavor-producing enzymes. Add a pinch of salt or slippery mineral-rich kelp for bitterness to balance the flavor. If vegetables darken, stir in a spoonful of vinegar, which stabilizes anthocyanin pigments. Rapid chilling and limiting air exposure prevent further quality loss.

Mitigating Advanced Over-Fermentation

For significantly over-fermented vegetables that lack crunch and bite, consider using them as a cooked ingredient in soups, stews, or sautés where texture flaws won't stand out.

Puree into dips and sauces to incorporate their intense sourness seamlessly. Mix small amounts with fresh, less-fermented ingredients like shredded carrots and cabbage to create coleslaw. Pair with fatty, sweet, or strongly flavored ingredients that balance and mask acidity. With care, you can adapt accidentally mushy ferments into new palatable formats.

Learning from Over-Fermenting

Make adjustments to avoid repeating over-fermentation by reassessing recipes and fermentation duration guidelines since over-fermenting suggests the timeframes are too long. Consider ambient temperatures and whether the fermentation environment is too warm, speeding the process.

If high acidity was the issue, incorporate more salt in the next round within prescribed limits to slow acid production. Determine if vessel and vegetable ratios allowed too much exposure to accumulating acids. Pinpoint where variables differed from successful batches and target the likely miscalculations or environmental factors.

Troubleshooting Insufficient Brine

One common cause of under and over-fermentation is inadequate protective brine. Always start with ample brine to fully submerge vegetables, preventing surface mold growth. Use recommended salt percentages to reliably draw moisture from the veggies into the surrounding brine. Weight vegetables to keep them immersed to stop them from floating up into airspace as fermentation proceeds.

If the brine recedes, add reserved initial brine from fermentation or new brine to restore coverage. For salt-only ferments, like sauerkraut, sprinkle extra salt on top to draw out more juices if needed. Sufficient brine is required throughout the entire fermentation period for safety and quality.

Troubleshooting Spoiled Batches

If a batch goes irrevocably bad despite your best efforts, promptly discard any ferment displaying dark mold within the jar or soft rotted vegetables to avoid contamination risks. Do not taste risky foods. Toss out ferments with pronounced off-odors, like strong ammonia, yeast, or decomposition. Rely on your senses.

Don't attempt to rescue batches left too long at room temperature if mold gets a foothold before lactic acid takes hold. If mold recurs despite sanitizing, reevaluate the entire preparation process and fermentation environment. Don't compromise safety by attempting to salvage or conceal spoiled foods. Some batches can't be redeemed.

Learning from Total Failures

While disposing of an unsalvageable batch may sting, view it as a valuable lesson. Carefully review recipes and processes from ingredients through the final steps to identify where errors likely occurred. Compare recipes and procedures to your past successful batches to pinpoint differences that led to failure. Make exacting notes on recipes, salt quantities, temperatures, durations, observations, and variations to inform future efforts. Research and enlist guidance from experienced fermenters to clarify where things went wrong. With a constructive assessment, the loss still brings valuable insights to create consistently tasty and safe ferments.

Problematic ferments don't have to mean defeat. Many wayward batches can get back on track with minimal intervention by quickly identifying temperature, time, contamination, or other issues. Even inedible results provide the opportunity for revelations. With careful tweaking of variables and troubleshooting techniques, your ferments will reliably achieve the flavors, textures, and preservative properties you desire.

Chapter 8: Beyond Basics: Showcasing Your Fermented Creations

You've mastered the art of lacto-fermentation and now have jars filled with tangy homemade sauerkraut, pickles, kimchi, and more. But what's next after the fermenting fun? This chapter goes beyond the basics and explores fun ways to showcase your fermented masterpieces creatively.

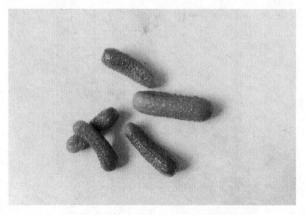

15. Explore ways to showcase your fermented masterpieces. Source: https://www.pexels.com/photo/cucumber-pickles-on-white-surface-8601704/

You'll discover ideas for aesthetically presenting ferments to highlight their visual appeal. You'll learn simple ways to share your signature recipes and fermenting knowledge with excited friends and family. And you'll examine how embracing fermentation as a hobby can support a sustainable and flavorful lifestyle.

Presenting Your Fermented Vegetables Aesthetically

You've mastered lacto-fermentation and have jars brimming with tangy homemade sauerkraut, pickles, kimchi, and more. But how can you make your fermented vegetable creations look as bold and vibrant as they taste? Here is how to elevate the eye-catching appeal of your preserved handcrafted bounty.

Plating Techniques for Show-Stopping Visual Impact

Artful plating can instantly take your humble fermented creations to the next level. Here are some techniques to try that can help your ferments stand out:

- Strategically use contrasting colors on the plate to grab people's attention. For example, mound bright pink kraut or curtido salad on top of dark leafy greens. The color pop draws the eye. Or sprinkle golden sautéed carrots atop a bed of purple cabbage sauerkraut. Vibrant reds layered on greens create an appetizing color contrast.

- Play with the different heights and shapes of the components you add to the plate. Rather than keeping everything uniformly flat and evenly distributed, create interest by mounding the sauerkraut or pickled vegetables into a tall heap or small pile off to the side. Whether loosely rounded or neatly compacted, varying the heights adds dimension.

- Instead of crowding the plate, intentionally leave negative space around focal items to let them stand out. Allow the star-pickled element breathing room. Resist the urge to surround it too closely with other components.

- Zigzag vibrantly colored pickled veggie brines over the plate in alternating directions for a dynamic look. Drizzle creatively rather than haphazardly. Consider making a zigzagged, quick pickled beet or carrot brine vinaigrette to liven up the plate artistically.

- Play with artfully arranging and alternating the placement of different pickled vegetables, cured meats, and cheeses attractively on the plate, whether lining them end-to-end in a row or wedging and weaving them together for an interlocked effect.

- Combine different textures, like a creamy element and crunchy pickles. Top tangy yogurt or ricotta with crisp fermented veggies for contrast. The possibilities are endless for adding textural variety through a mix-and-match presentation.

With some thoughtful placement organization, you can make your humble ferments look polished, professional, and irresistible. Artfully composed plates transform homemade into haute cuisine.

Unique Ways to Serve Up Your Fermented Delights

For an unexpected and interactive presentation, consider serving your fermented vegetables creatively:

- Scoop out vegetables like ripe tomatoes, bell peppers, or avocados and fill the edible vessels with your colorful pickled creations, nestling them on a bed of fresh salad greens or pasta for added support.

- Wrap individual portions of shredded pickled vegetables tightly, like summer rolls, in large outer lettuce or cabbage leaves for portable fermented wraps.

- Alternate pieces of pickled vegetables, cheeses, and fresh or dried fruits like apricots and apples on frilly toothpicks or skewers for a fun, stacked look.

- Mash egg yolks and mix them with your favorite fermented vegetable. Then, spoon the mixture into halved hard-boiled egg whites for an inventive egg salad presentation.

- Top halved baked russet or sweet potatoes with sauerkraut, pickled onions, cheese, and bacon, like loaded fermented potato skins ready for baking.

- Place heaps or slices of your homemade pickles on individual toasted baguette slices, crostini, or crackers for easy open-faced pickled appetizers or snacks.

- Serve pickle shots of straight-up fermented brine or brine mixed with veggie juices for fun pickleback drinks.

The possibilities are endless when you think outside the jar. Unique vessels and presentations make enjoying your fermented fare interactive and memorable.

Tips and Tricks for Optimizing the Visual Appeal of Colors

Vibrant colors instantly make dishes leap off the plate. Here are some ways to use colors for maximum eye-catching impact:

- Spotlight the signature vibrant hues of natural foods like ruby red cabbage sauerkraut or golden pickled carrots. Pair with contrasting dark leafy greens like spinach or kale to make their colors pop even more.

- Lacto-ferment produce that is naturally colorful when raw, like golden beets, vibrant purple cabbage, or rainbow carrots. Their pigments will brighten up any dish.

- Use fresh, vibrant herb garnishes like chopped parsley, cilantro, or chives. Their bursts of green instantly enliven a plate.

- Add thin slices of raw vegetables like cucumber, radish, or fennel for color contrast. Or use micro greens like pea tendrils or beet greens.

- Incorporate spices like turmeric, sweet paprika, or saffron into your ferments. Their sunset hues add natural beauty.

- Blend up fermented hot sauces with red bell peppers, sun-dried tomatoes, or carrot juice for rich orange and red tones.

Vivid colors naturally make people excited to taste your tasty, fermented creations. Leverage produce's vivid natural hues to create an appetizing palette.

Ways to Showcase Texture Variety for Maximum Appeal

Including a mix of diversely textured components can further heighten visual and taste appeal:

- Highlight your ferments' signature crunch by slicing vegetables paper thin into matchsticks or shreds to maximize their crisp texture.

- Toast crackers like flaxseed or multigrain and top with soft creamy cheese and crispy fermented vegetable shreds for contrast.

- Use a scoop of your favorite ferment, like curtido or kimchi, to top tender proteins like grilled salmon, roasted chicken, or silky scrambled eggs. The pickles' crunch provides textural contrast.

- In grain bowls or on dinner plates, combine the raw, crunchy texture of ferments with smooth, creamy mashed root vegetables, like sweet potatoes or carrots.

- Leave pickled fruits like grapes, chopped plums, or berries partially whole and barely broken down for an intriguing tender-crisp textural combination.

- Dip crispy endive leaves, apple slices, or crackers into sauces or vinaigrettes made with brine from fermented jalapenos, carrots, or green tomatoes for a hit of acid and crunch in each scooping bite.

Playing with textural components excites the palate and makes dishes even more craveable. Capitalize on your ferments' natural textures through thoughtful pairing.

Decorative Touches to Add That Finishing Flair

A few artful decorative touches can add the final flair that makes your fermented presentation pop:

- Shave or slice fermented vegetables like cucumbers, radishes, or beets into delicate ribbons or paper-thin slices as garnish. Their colorful, frilly edges make any plate or drink more elegant.

- Add whole, unique spices, like black peppercorns, fennel, or nigella seeds. Allow their interesting shapes and colors to accent the plate.

- Make whimsical mini skewers by carefully skewering small, pickled vegetable pieces, fresh herb leaves, edible flowers, or ripe fruits onto frilly toothpicks.

- Get creative with height and shape by using ingredients like crisp fried shallots, capers still on their stems, or finely slivered pickled red onions or jalapenos.

- Garnish dishes with edible flowers like nasturtium, borage, pansies, or pea shoots. Their natural beauty jazzes up any presentation.

- For pickleback shots, fashionably rim glassware with chili flakes, smoked paprika, or coarsely cracked black pepper.

Even small, skillfully placed accents can take your presentation over the top. Have fun enhancing dishes with artful edible garnishes.

Unique Vessels to Complement and Highlight Your Creations

Serve your fermented creations in or on vessels that complement their vibrant colors and textures:

- Scoop out ripened fruit like avocados and stuff with kraut salad. Hollowed tomatoes or shallots make surprising edible vessels.

- Use attractive boards, plates, or platters made of natural materials like wood, stone, or slate. Their neutrality lets the ferments take center stage.

- Bright white rectangular plates provide a crisp, clean backdrop to make colors pop. Classic white dishware never goes out of style.

- Clear glass stemless wine glasses, mini mason jars, or shot glasses show off fermented compositions and brine colors through the transparent walls.

- Metallic finishes, like untreated copper, silver, or gold, add glamour, while earthy, unglazed pottery or porcelain provide handmade rustic appeal.

Choose serving pieces that complement your creation. Then, let the vibrant beauty of your ferments shine.

Composing a Stunning Fermented Vegetable Charcuterie Board

For an impressive appetizer spread, artfully compose a fermented vegetable charcuterie board featuring:

- Begin with an attractive wood board in a circular or rectangular shape. Arrange small clusters of various fermented items, like kraut, curtido, kimchi, pickled vegetables, tapenades, fermented salsas, and hot sauces.

- Incorporate crunchy crackers, crunchy rustic bread slices, toasted nuts, or crispy chickpeas for a delightful textural contrast. Add thin slices of cured or roasted meats like prosciutto, salami, sausages, or chicken.

- For balance, include creamy elements, like soft cheeses, labneh, thick Greek yogurt, or white bean dip. Add fresh fruits, like apples, pears, fig slices, grapes, dates, and dried apricots or raisins to provide sweetness.

- Fill in gaps with petite sprigs of fresh herbs, like dill, fennel fronds, rosemary, or thyme. Olives, cornichons, edible flowers, and micro greens provide the finishing touches.

A thoughtfully composed board makes your ferments the star while providing guests with an artful variety of components to enjoy together. Elevate your preserved creations to a whole new level.

You can transform humble fermented vegetables into an elegant, enticing culinary presentation with creativity, skillful plating techniques, unique serving ideas, decorative touches, and vessels. Have fun playing with colors, textures, shapes, and arrangements to highlight the natural beauty of your homemade fermented bounty. Before you know it, your creations will be the talk of the table.

Sharing Your Recipes with Friends and Family

You've become passionate about lacto-fermentation and pickling, filling your pantry with tasty homemade sauerkraut, pickles, relishes, and more. Naturally, you want to spread the joy by sharing your fermenting and pickling recipes with lucky friends and family. Here's how you can do it.

Recipe Formatting Tips

To make your recipes easy for others to follow, use this format:

- **Title**: Choose a fun, descriptive recipe name.

- **Ingredient List**: Comprehensively list all ingredients in order of use and the precise measurements.

- **Equipment List**: Note special equipment needed, like fermentation weights, jars, etc.

- **Step-by-Step Instructions**: Write clear, thorough directions anyone can follow. Explain fermentation troubleshooting tips.

- **Storage Notes**: Include expected shelf life for fermented items and storage recommendations.

- **Recipe Source**: Credit yourself or where you adapted it from.

A well-formatted recipe allows friends to recreate your fermented masterpieces successfully.

Writing Clear Fermenting Directions

Since the fermentation process involves special steps, like brine ratios, fermenting times, and troubleshooting, be extra clear in your instructions:

- Carefully explain how to make brines, including precise salt-to-water ratios and seasonings. Note weights, measurements, and water amounts.

- Specify fermenting duration, temperatures, and signs of readiness based on your experience. Explain the variables like climate differences.

- Describe in detail how to pack jars, submerge vegetables, and safely release gases during fermentation.

- Explain what's normal in fermentation, like scum formation, yeast blooms, bubble release, etc., so they know the troubleshooting signs. Alleviate intimidation factors.

Thorough, encouraging instructions give new fermenters confidence. They'll be more likely to attempt your recipes successfully.

Gifts from the Ferment

Sharing your fermented bounty edibles makes a heartfelt gift:

- Assemble a homemade fermenting cookbook with your favorite recipes. Include photos and personal tips.

- Create a fermentation toolkit with your recipes as a gift with essential supplies, like weights, jars, gloves, and salts.

- Gift jars of your signature sauerkrauts, pickles, kimchis, and relishes labeled with personalized tags and instructions.

- Make herb blends, brines, or pickling spice mixes tailored to your recipes to give with them.

- Pair recipes with fermented food gifts like kimchi pancakes or pickle gift baskets.

- Host a pickled potluck party: Ask friends and family to share recipes and creations.

Gifting your fermented foods lets others experience homemade flavors while spreading recipes you perfected.

Host a Hands-on Fermenting Party

For complete fermenting immersion, host a hands-on fermenting party:

- Plan a theme like kimchi-making or pickling. Have the required vegetables and equipment ready.

- Provide detailed step-by-step recipe handouts for guests to follow and explain each step verbally.

- As they follow along, share tips you learned to avoid common troubleshooting issues.

- Let guests customize flavors and get creative as they gain confidence.

- At the end, enjoy tasting samples together. Have them vote on favorites.

An immersive fermenting party removes intimidation factors, so guests gain a first-hand preserving experience.

Digitally Sharing Recipes

You can also generously share recipes digitally:

- Email your personalized recipes as attachments to friends and family who express interest.

- Post recipes step-by-step on social media and invite questions in comments from followers.

- Create a blog dedicated to your fermenting recipes and tips. Help spread your passion.

- Contribute recipes to online recipe sites and forums for fermenting and pickling aficionados.

- Create video tutorials explaining your techniques and walking through recipes to share on YouTube.

Digital platforms allow you to spread fermenting inspiration worldwide to motivate and educate fellow food DIY enthusiasts.

Many options exist for generously sharing your fermenting and pickling know-how. Whether through gifting homemade items, hands-on workshops, or virtual recipes, you can thoughtfully impart your knowledge to help your loved ones discover the joys of fermenting for themselves. Spread the bubbling briny love.

Embracing a Sustainable and Flavorful Lifestyle through Fermentation

You've grown to love the flavors and health benefits of homemade fermented foods like sauerkraut, kimchi, and pickles. An exciting lifestyle possibility is discovering more ways fermentation skills can support sustainable, flavorful living.

Here are some ideas for embracing fermentation as a hobby while enhancing sustainability, saving money, reducing waste, and enjoying homemade flavors.

Growing Some of What You Ferment

Consider growing some of the fresh vegetables you plan to ferment in a garden, raised beds, or pots.

Cultivate cabbage, cucumbers, carrots, beets, other root veggies, tomatoes, peppers, greens, herbs, and more. Choose heirloom varieties boasting enhanced nutrients, colors, and flavors. Plant produce earlier than usual, so it's ready for prime seasonal fermenting. Stagger plantings to ensure continuous harvest for ferments.

Save seeds from top performers to plant again. Trade seeds with other local gardeners. Share or sell your surplus crop at farmers' markets. Gardening provides sustainably grown, local ingredients at their peak freshness for fermenting. Reduce food miles while getting active outdoors.

Preserving the Season's Bounty

Preserve abundant crops at their seasonal prime through fermentation:

- As fruits and vegetables ripen, assess what you can consume fresh and what's optimal for fermenting.

- Move quickly to pickle peak produce like cucumbers and summer squash within hours of harvesting. Speed preserves nutrition.

- Batch prepare recipes when you have a windfall crop like cabbage, peppers, or carrots. Stock up your pantry.

- Vary your fermented creations depending on the available seasonal bounty. Try new flavors based on what's ripe.

Harness fermentation's power to capture seasonal flavors and nutrition instead of losing surplus to waste.

Reducing Food Waste through Fermentation

Ferment overripe or imperfect produce that would otherwise get tossed:

- Transform bruised tomatoes, overripe stone fruit, or blemished apples into fermented condiments, like ketchup, chutneys, and fruit krauts.

- Pickle the ends, peels, tops, and outer leaves of vegetables destined for compost, like beet greens, carrot tops, and heartier outer cabbage leaves. Waste not.

- Revive limp veggies by quickly infusing them with life through lacto-fermentation. Even aging produce retains nutrients.

See the possibilities in imperfect produce. Let fermentation give forgotten food a new purpose.

Getting Economical with Fermented Staples

Stretch grocery bills by fermenting inexpensive basics into flavor-packed staples:

- Turn cheap cabbage into tangy, probiotic-rich sauerkraut. Bulk pickle cucumbers in season.

- Transform value produce like carrots, beets, onions, and potatoes into lively ferments.

- Use whey leftovers from making yogurt or cheese as a probiotic starter for ferments. Waste becomes a resource.

- Frequent farmers' markets for deals on bulk or ugly duckling produce destined for fermentation greatness.

- Practice thrift and self-reliance by creatively fermenting humble staples into new delicacies.

Discovering More Fermentation Methods

Look beyond vegetables to expand your fermenting skills:

- Try culturing dairy into yogurt, kefir, cheese, and butter for flavorful probiotics.

- Brew kombucha, jun, or beet kvass, ferment tea, honey, or produce tangy tonics.

- Explore traditional dishes globally like kimchi, miso, and injera that rely on fermentation. Recreate them yourself.

- Ferment beans, nuts, and condiments, like soy sauce, almond milk yogurt, and garum fish sauce.

Keep seeking new fermentation frontiers. Let traditional methods inspire your own twists.

Conclusion

You made it through this ultimate guide on fermenting vegetables. Give yourself a nice pat on the back. From the beginning to the end, you've gained much knowledge and developed serious fermentation skills.

In the introduction, you learned why fermented foods are great for you - think probiotics for gut health, better digestion, and immunity. Plus, ferments add awesome flavor and texture to meals. The book aimed to make fermentation approachable and fun. Mission accomplished, right?

In this book, you learned that fermentation uses friendly lactobacilli bacteria to work through lacto-fermentation. Sauerkraut, kimchi, pickles - all transformed by natural fermentation and the associated health benefits. Understanding the science behind it gives you control over the process.

The book enlightened you with the essential tools and ingredients to ferment at home. You're now a pro at picking the right equipment and quality veggies. A sprinkle of salt here, a splash of brine there, you've got this. Safety first, though.

Moreover, you got hands-on with basic fermentation techniques. Following each step showed you how salt, temperature, and time impact the result. Whipping up some beginner recipes lets you put your new skills into practice.

Additionally, the book opened the door to the world of quick pickling with vinegar. You can easily infuse brines with different spices and flavors to make pickled creations your own. It's less fuss than fermenting but still deliciously fun.

By the middle of the book, you confidently fermented an array of veggies following foolproof recipes, from sauerkraut to kimchi and more. You can now control flavor profiles and craft ferments to suit your taste buds. Adding your homemade items to meals brought everything together.

Moving on, you leveled up your fermentation game with advanced techniques. Experimenting with different veggie and flavor combos lets you customize to your heart's content. Fine-tuning time and temperature takes your ferments to the next level. Your fermentation skills are now epic.

Additionally, the book helped you troubleshoot fermentation issues like mold or funky bacteria. You can now salvage batches by tweaking salt, spices, and time. Consider yourself a fermentation problem-solving guru.

By the end of the book, you could beautifully showcase your mouthwatering fermented creations. Spread the fermentation love by sharing tasty treats with family and friends. It's a great excuse to show off.

In short, you now have superior fermentation abilities. From start to finish, you learned techniques from basic to advanced. You understand the science behind it and can handle anything that comes up. Most importantly, your upgraded kitchen skills let you whip up endless fermented masterpieces.

Ultimately, don't doubt yourself. You can make fabulous, fermented foods at home. While starting, fermentation may have seemed intimidating. But you got in and discovered it is super satisfying and rewarding. Let your creativity run wild with new flavor combos, trusting your tastebuds to guide you. The possibilities are endless.

References

Daniel, Y. (2023a). Pickling and Fermenting Cookbook for Preppers: The Art and Science of Fermentation: Techniques for Preparing Probiotic Foods. XinXii.

Daniel, Y. (2023b). Pickling and Fermenting Cookbook for Preppers: The Prepper's Cookbook: Pickling and Fermenting Recipes for Sustainable Living. XinXii.

Feifer, A. (2015). Ferment Your Vegetables: A Fun and Flavorful Guide to Making Your Own Pickles, Kimchi, Kraut, and More. Fair Winds Press.

Huang, T. (2017). The Fermented Vegetables Manual: Enjoy Krauts, Pickles, and Kimchis the Right Way to Improve Skin, Health, and Happiness.

Kaufmann, K., & Schoneck, A. (2017). Making Sauerkraut and Pickled Vegetables at Home. Books Alive.

McVicker, K. (2020). Essential Vegetable Fermentation: 70 Inventive Recipes to Make Your Own Pickles, Kraut, Kimchi, and More. Sourcebooks, Inc.

Neil, M. H. (2016). Pickling - A How-to Guide with Recipes for the Pickling of Fruit and Vegetables. Read Books Ltd.

Park, K., Jk, J., Ye, L., & Daily, J. W. (2014). Health Benefits of Kimchi (Korean Fermented Vegetables) as a Probiotic Food. Journal of Medicinal Food, 17(1), 6–20.

Poffley, S., & Smolinska-Poffley, G. (2016). Ferment, Pickle, Dry: Ancient Methods, Modern Meals. Frances Lincoln

Made in the USA
Las Vegas, NV
21 February 2024

86048833R00107